LONDON'S LOST GLOBAL GIANT

In search of the East India Company

Roger Williams

Published in the UK by Bristol Book Publishing
www.bristolbook.co.uk

London's Lost Global Giant
ISBN: 978-0-9928466-2-6

Typeset in Plantin and Trade Gothic
Printed and bound in the UK by
Printondemand, Peterborough
www.printondemand-worldwide.com

LONDON'S
LOST
GLOBAL GIANT

THE LONDON TRILOGY

THE TEMPLES OF LONDON
Inspired architecture

FATHER THAMES
Stories from the incoming tide

LONDON'S LOST GLOBAL GIANT
In search of the East India Company

Other books by Roger Williams

Non-fiction
The Fisherman of Halicarnassus
The Royal Albert Hall:
a Victorian Masterpiece for the 21st Century
London Top 10
The Most Amazing Places to Visit in London (co-author)
Royal London (illustrations by John Cleave)
Eyewitness Barcelona and *Provence*
Berlitz Dubrovnik and *Tenerife*
& many other travel books and guides

Fiction
Aftermath
A-Train
Burning Barcelona
High Times at the Hotel Bristol
Lunch with Elizabeth David
All fiction titles are available as ebooks

For Annie

Acknowledgements

My thanks to Natasha Bennett at the Royal Armouries,
Ian Denning, Philip Dröge, Chris Ellmers at the
Museum of London Docklands, David Iggulden at the
Royal Botanic Gardens Kew, Margaret Makepeace at
the British Library, Claire Penhallurick at Bonhams,
Emma Rogers at the V&A, Ann Sylph at the Zoological
Society of London, Justine Taylor at the Honourable
Artillery Company and Edward Weech at the Royal
Asiatic Society. And to Pam Barrett and Rose Shepherd
for their discerning editorial eyes.

CONTENTS

JOHN COMPANY

On a bright Saturday morning in May 2007, the East Indiaman *Götheborg* sailed between the raised bascules of Tower Bridge to arrive in the Upper Pool of London. It was an historic moment. *Götheborg* fired her cannon in a salute that was returned by the guns of HMS *Belfast*, the first time they had sounded since the Second World War battle cruiser had arrived at her berth in Southwark thirty-six years earlier. But it was the world's largest working wooden sailing ship that caused the excitement. The full-scale replica of an 18th-century East Indiaman was returning from China on her maiden voyage from her native Sweden, and visitors were invited to clamber aboard when she docked at South Quay in Canary Wharf before returning to her home port of Gothenburg two weeks later. Souvenirs that she took from her visit to London included plants from the Chelsea Flower Show where a special Swedish garden had been designed that year to celebrate the tercentenary of the birth of Carl Linnaeus, the Swedish botanist who, like so many eminent men of his day, had a deep interest in the discoveries and bounty of the India trade.

The replica *Götheborg*, entirely modern within, had arrived in the city of the Honourable East India Company, sometimes known as John Company, whose mighty cargo ships, guns bristling, holds bulging, once dominated world trade. It had been exactly 150 years since the Indian Mutiny had precipitated its downfall, and an East Indiaman had not been seen in London in well over a century.

Sweden was one of several European countries to instigate a national charter company with exclusive trading rights to the spice-rich lands and islands of Asia. The sea route had been opened by the Portuguese explorer Vasco da Gama in 1499, a century before the East India Company was formed in London. Portugal went on to establish trading posts for its empire in India and China, but an attempt to set up a joint-stock company, the Companhia da Índia Oriental, in 1628, quickly petered out. Denmark had two attempts at creating companies, in 1616 and 1670. But it was the French and the Dutch who were England's main competition. The Compagnie Française des Indes Orientales, established in 1664 by Louis XIV's chief minister Colbert, was given the chop in the French Revolution. More successful was the Vereenigde Oostindische Compagnie in the Netherlands, lasting from 1602 to 1799. John Company, formed two years earlier and enduring a lingering death in the 19th century, outlasted them all.

A royal charter granting the use of the word 'honourable' is not given lightly. In 2014, shortly before Prince William took up a position with an air ambulance service, the Guild of Air Pilots, based in Gray's Inn, was granted the title, joining two other companies in London: the Honourable Artillery Company and the Honourable Merchant Mariners Company. The HAC is Britain's oldest regiment. It was given its charter by Henry VIII in 1537. Created to keep the City safe, it was called out to help quell riots, such as those among the Spitalfields weavers angered by the East India Company's cheap imports of calico. Its headquarters are in extensive grounds behind an unexpected Victorian Gothic castle in City Road, and it remains a volunteer regiment of the Army Reserve, its members serving in world conflicts as well as supplying costumed pikemen to attend the Lord Mayor in his golden coach and on his visits to the City's livery halls. There was no livery company for sailors of the East India Company to join, and it was not until 1925 that the Honourable Company of Merchant Mariners was granted the title by George V. HQS *Wellington*, moored on the Thames at Temple Pier, was donated by the Royal Navy to become their headquarters and London's only floating livery hall.

But of the Honourable East India Company there is no sign: no livery hall, no parade ground, no replica ships, no flags, no re-enactments or dressing up, no heritage sites. The *Götheborg* flew her colours, fired guns and courted praise before returning to Gothenburg where the former headquarters of the Swedish East India Company remains an imposing landmark in a prime site by the Grand Harbour

Canal. Since 1861 it has housed the City Museum, and the reconstructed auction room has a permanent exhibition about the Company, which was co-founded by a Scot, Colin Campbell, and carried out much of its trading with Canton in China.

In Holland, too, the old VOC headquarters is a canalside landmark, and not one but two full-size Dutch replica East India cargo ships can be visited. But in London there is little to see of what had been, for much of its 250 years, the biggest company in the world. Ignored in the square mile of the City, which it once dominated, it does occasionally surface elsewhere. Its story is now told in the National Maritime Museum's Traders Gallery, and the company name has been revived by an enterprising Indian businessman. The Honourable East India Company otherwise seems to have sunk with barely a trace.

A century after it was founded in 1600, its London office had only thirty-five employees, yet another century on and it had a private army of 260,000 and the largest shipping fleet, as well as the largest docks, in the world. With many acres of buildings, it was the capital's biggest employer: 4,000 worked in its docks, warehouses and offices, and 35,000 Londoners are reckoned to have relied on the Company for a living, with a further 25,000 countrywide. The Company poured money into the royal coffers, made the sons of working men rich, helped to fuel the industrial revolution and gave the nation a taste for the Orient and an addiction to tea. It was also corrupt, exploitative and perilous. The British

Association for Cemeteries in South Asia looks after an estimated two million graves and monuments of British and other Europeans between the Red Sea and the China coast – *"wherever the East India Company and its rivals from France, the Netherlands and Denmark set foot"*. There are no graves for those who died at sea. The Company set up asylums in India and one in Hackney for employees who had been driven insane.

Successive generations have seen opinion sharply divided on the legacy and impact of the Company that was deemed too big to fail. In *The Corporation that Changed the World* the London financier Nick Robins is unstinting in his easy comparisons with contemporary corporate evil: *"For me, the parallels with today's leviathans soon became overpowering, with the Company outstripping Walmart in terms of market power, Enron for corruption and Union Carbide for human devastation."*

Yet no empire was ever forged without exploitation, without crimes against humanity and the shedding of blood; nor has a company ever grown seriously rich without powerful, overriding self-interest. Other writers and historians have seen much that was beneficial and positive in the Company. Curiosity and a thirst for knowledge as well as genuinely held good will and a wish to instil honest business practice and make the world a better place could be found among those heading for the East. Many ordinary people living in Britain today have stories about their forebears' connections with India or China, connections that add a splash of welcome glamour to their background.

The Company's India was a vast and often mysterious place. The word 'Indian' comes from the Greek and Latin names for anybody living beyond the River Indus, and the Company sometimes used the word with a similar grand sweep, even applying it to Australia. 'India' meant everything exotic in the East, and to travel there was without doubt a great adventure that led many extraordinary men and women to wonderful worlds and eye-opening encounters. To some, it was a kind of Klondike, to others it was an education. For many it was simply a means of escape. It fired the imaginations of young men throughout the country. Lord Byron, aged twenty-one, contemplated a journey to India. *"If I do not travel now, I never shall; and all men should one day or other,"* he wrote to his mother from Newstead Abbey on November 2, 1808. He hoped to be sailing the following March, he told her. But nobody was permitted on a ship heading for Asia without the Company's approval, which he failed to obtain. The difficulty of reaching India can only have added to its mystery and attraction.

Queen Elizabeth I had unleashed England's sea dogs on to the high seas to start an empire, and she launched the Honourable East India Company, too. Their spirit of enterprise and adventure, their ability to create waves, has sailed down the centuries, and there is no better way to understand their appeal than the sight of a tall ship, which *Götheborg* provided as she tied up on the Thames. The attraction of those days of sail has not disappeared. What has been lost is an awareness that the Honourable East India Company, such a crucial ingredient in Britain's prosperity and culture, was ever in London at all.

EAST INDIA HOUSE

Richard Rogers' bold glass and stainless steel Lloyd's building is the youngest in the country to be given a Grade I listing, although it shocked the City when it was completed in 1986. Equally shocking was the disappearance of a building on the same site more than a hundred years earlier. If it had survived another hundred years, it would certainly have been designated a listed building, and the insurance institution's headquarters would never have found space here.

East India House was a London landmark, a dramatic neoclassical showpiece for the greatest company the world had ever known. After the Honourable East India Company ceased trading in 1857, it was pulled down, its employees pensioned off,

its masonry recycled, its treasures scattered to the four winds. The City has no time for sentiment. Losers simply disappear.

The 'Monster of Leadenhall Street' had a 200-metre frontage decorated with statues that reinforced its view as the controller of world trade with a monopoly everywhere east of the Cape of Good Hope. Inside, business was determined by the twenty-four-strong Court of Directors, elected annually by the shareholders known as the Court of the Proprietors and headed by a Governor chosen among themselves. A warren of lamplit corridors led to a diversity of offices, but so well ordered was it that visitors from Bombay dockyards in the late 1830s remarked that not a soul was to be seen, in spite of the hundreds who worked there, and they worried they might not find their own way out of the "passages and windings".

In the grander rooms and on staircases there were pictures and statues that told the story of the Company's success. The Court Room, a large cubic space thirty feet long, wide and high, was hung with paintings of its domains: the three Indian Presidencies of Bengal, Madras and Bombay, the Atlantic island of St Helena and South Africa's Cape, while the Finance and Home Committee Room had a fanciful picture of *The Grant of the Dewanee to Lord Clive and the Company* in 1765, the historic event that gave the Company power to collect all the revenues in Bengal, and so secured its control over India. The most raucous of rooms, described as a 'bear pit', was the great Sale Room where cargoes were auctioned, and among the quietest were the museum and library with the greatest collection of works about India.

The Company sustained many businesses around Leadenhall Street where there were stationers, publishers, pocket-book sellers, gunsmiths, trunk makers, 'chinamen', grocers, chemists and drapers. The Two Fans was an 'India House', selling Japan wares, silks, tea and arrack. At No.8 was Parbury & Co and the Oriental Herald Office, a specialist in books on the East, with a short-lived monthly publication, the *Oriental Herald*. A painted wooden figure of a naval lieutenant in dress uniform outside No.157 flagged a nautical instrument maker: Company men were expected to buy their own. At No.36, then 105, the marine painter William John Huggins, R.A., had a studio. He had sailed with the Company to China and his pictures of East Indiamen were popular among the mariners who came to East India House to pick up their wages, to deliver ships' logs and reports on their journeys. The street's best known hostelry was the Ship and Turtle Tavern, at No.129, serving some of the best turtle soup in London to, among others, the Masons who held lodge meetings here. Advancement through the Company could be helped through Freemasonry, which reached India in 1730.

When East India House was sold along with its furniture, fixtures and fittings, many people went out of business. After decades of expansion, the Company had suffered a lingering death, coming under a government Board of Control in 1794, then losing its monopolies, first in India in 1813, then China in 1833. Finally, in 1858, as a direct result of the Indian Mutiny, it was taken into the British Empire; Queen Victoria was crowned India's Empress, and the British Raj (Hindu for 'rule') took up the reins. A rising tide of events had overtaken the Company and washed away 257 years of history.

It had begun in Elizabethan times with the meeting of merchants who had an interest in trading. A popular place for those with an interest in Asia was the Nag's Head Inn in Bishopsgate, but after their royal charter was granted in 1600, the Honourable East India Company found a more suitable address in the house of its first governor, Sir Thomas Smythe, around whom London's mercantile world turned. Smythe's father had been a 'customer', overseeing shipments in the Port of London, and Sir Thomas had a finger in many 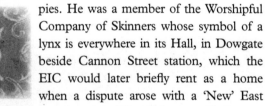 pies. He was a member of the Worshipful Company of Skinners whose symbol of a lynx is everywhere in its Hall, in Dowgate beside Cannon Street station, which the EIC would later briefly rent as a home when a dispute arose with a 'New' East India Company in 1698. The Skinners still disperse funds endowed by a trust set up with Smythe's fortunes. His own house in Philpot Lane, between Eastcheap and Fenchurch Street where the 'Walkie Talkie' now stands, was always abuzz with gossip and news from merchants, traders, explorers, investors and sea captains. Wives would come in search of news, beds were made available, instruction was given in navigation, new waters were charted, and there was a collection of curiosities from around the known world. An Inuit kayak hung from the beams of the Great Hall, which was used by the Muscovy Company, formed by Smythe's grandfather in 1555, and the Levant Company (1581), in both of which he had an interest, as he would soon have in the Virginia Company (1606). It was therefore natural that the East India Company met here, too, and this is where it remained for twenty-one years, until Smythe, aged sixty-three and two years from death, stepped down because of failing health.

The hall in Smythe's house is thought to have been similar to the one in Crosby House, Bishopsgate, which the Company chose for its base for the following seventeen years. Built by a wool merchant, Sir John Crosby, its tenants included Richard III when he was Duke of Gloucester. It later became part of the estate of Sir Thomas More, in whose footsteps it followed in 1910 when its magnificent Hall, which was all that remained, was removed to Cheyne Walk in Chelsea where More, Chancellor to Henry VIII, once had a farm. The work was organised under the London County Council and paid for by the Bank of India, recently founded in Bombay, which took over the Bishopsgate site. In Chelsea an Arts and Crafts block was added to the Hall, and when the Greater London Council was abolished in 1988, it went up for sale. Its buyer was Christopher Moran, as buccaneering a figure as any East India venturer, who would later broker the sale of the Conservative Central Office for Margaret Thatcher. Born in north London, he made his first million by the age of twenty-one, and has been censured by the London Stock Exchange, barred by Lloyd's and fined $2 million for insider trading in the USA.

With advice from English Heritage, among others, Moran created a thirty-bedroom home in a magnificent private Tudor-style palace with an entrance range based on Hampton Court and a period courtyard garden. The Hall, fully restored, has been described as *"the most important surviving secular domestic Medieval building in London"*.

CARGOES

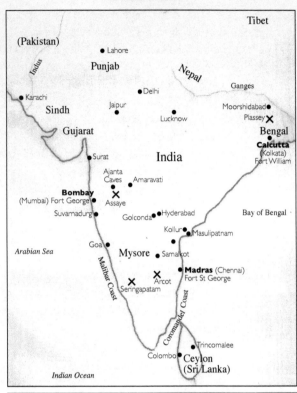

SPICES

The promise of peppers and other spices is what first put the wind in the East India Company's sails. Since antiquity pepper had been an expensive and sought-after commodity. In the first century AD profits from a 200-ton shipment of Indian pepper would pay the wages of 6,000 Roman legionnaires for a year. In London not long after the Norman Conquest the Guild of Pepperers was established to ensure purity and to regulate weights and measures (*pesso grosso*) of not just peppers but all spices and medicinal plants. In the fourteenth century it changed its name to the Guild of Grossers or Grocers, while medicines were hived off to the Worshipful Company of Apothecaries.

Incorporated into the heraldic device of the Grocers' Company is the Pepperers' symbol of a camel, to show that their goods had come overland, via the Middle East and Istanbul where the colourful Spice Bazaar can still excite the most jaded palate. From Istanbul to Venice was a short hop, and with a monopoly on trade with Egypt, too, La Serenissima built its shimmering canal-side *palazzi* on fortunes made in the spice trade. Venice maintained a grip on European markets, sending galleys to the Netherlands and England in spring with exotic goods from Turkey, Persia and India. So when Vasco da Gama led the Portuguese around the Cape of Good Hope in 1497 to find spices and cut off the dozens of markets and middle men in between, the rest of Western Europe was eager to follow. The Dutch, whose ports enjoyed free trade, were not far behind, sailing to Java and to Moluccas, the source of cloves, mace and nutmegs, soon labelled 'the Spice Islands', in what today is Indonesia. The Dutch monopoly of the pepper trade was particularly frustrating, especially when the price began to rocket. The English were keen as other countries to have a slice of this business but they were late starters and had some catching up to do.

The commander of the Company's first voyage was James Lancaster, who should be better known. He had been 'brought up with the Portuguese' and fought alongside Sir Francis Drake against the Spanish before heading east, reaching Ceylon (Sri Lanka) and Malaya and attacking any foreign ship laden with goods. Like Governor Sir Thomas Smythe, Lancaster was a member of the Skinners' Company, where his fine portrait hangs, and where he is well remembered as he, too, grew rich enough to endow a lasting charitable trust. He was put in charge of the thirty-eight-gun *Red Dragon*, the largest of four vessels manned by a total crew of five hundred. In the five years since she had been built in Deptford for the Duke of Cumberland, the *Red Dragon* had been wreaking havoc among the Spanish in the Atlantic. Now in the employ of the East India Company, she would make a total of six voyages to the Indian Ocean, her guns ever ready to snatch ships' cargoes and keep rivals at bay.

Lancaster's fleet left London on February 13, 1601, and by the time it reached South Africa's

Cape a hundred crew had died through accident and illness, though Lancaster is reputed to be the first to have used lemons to combat scurvy. They returned after capturing several Portuguese ships and many other adventures on September 11, 1603, their holds filled with five hundred tons of pepper from Java where they had set up the Company's first factory, or trading post, in Bantham.

For the English sailors, these must have seemed overwhelmingly pungent lands. Down wind, it was said, cinnamon in Ceylon could be detected twenty-five miles out to sea. Once the spices were stashed on board, the ship would have smelled a great deal better than it had after months of men living in close quarters at sea.

Streets around the warehouses in London would soon become thick with the smell of spices, too. Among the last of these, and the largest warehouse complex on the river when it was completed in 1873, was Shad Thames on the south side of Tower Bridge, where aromas today rise from riverside restaurants. With cast-iron walkways used by porters linking Butler's Wharf warehouses to the  Cardamom Buildings behind, it survived the area's conversion at the end of the twentieth century from industrial use to smart residential flats. Though the buildings had been vacant for a decade or more, the aromas of spices had seeped so far into the brickwork that the first buyers could still smell them as they stood in their kitchens or tucked themselves up in bed. The blocks, or courts, are now named Cayenne,

Sesame, Vanilla and Tamarind, and the theme is milked by Clove Building, Anise Gallery and Bengal Clipper Indian restaurant. Beyond it, the lane turns inland beside Jacob's Island, a muddy creek where the Java Wharf looks as if it might still be shipping sacks full of pepper. Shad Thames offers the nearest sniff to be had of the city's spice-trading past.

None of these spices was new to the English table. What was new was their greater availability, and it was this that affected the national cuisine. In *Spices, Salt and Aromatics in the English Kitchen*, Elizabeth David points out that it was not until the middle of the seventeenth century, *"when the East India Company had become a power to be reckoned with, that English cooking began to develop along lines that we can recognise today"*.

Certainly it produced a love of spices, of nutmeg, cinnamon and cloves, in cakes and pies, in potted shrimps and warming drinks, and gentlemen often carried nutmegs and small graters, while silver shakers dispensed cinnamon onto toast and crumpets. Company men and their wives returning from the East may well have enjoyed Indian dishes, which they might attempt to have cooked for them, or even cooked themselves, back at home.

Hannah Glasse's 1714 *The Art of Cookery Made Plain and Easy* contained one of the first recipes for curry, in which only pepper and coriander seeds were added to spice a dish of chicken and rice. The book was popular for a century, going through several editions, and was published in facsimile form by Prospect Books in 1995. Pickles, sauces and soy-based catsup, or catshup, were among the earliest products to be appreciated on board ship because they had a long life and could flavour stored food.

In a chapter titled 'For Captains of Ships' Glasse gives a recipe for *Catshup to keep Twenty Years*. The ingredients are mace, cloves, ginger, mushrooms, anchovies and 'stale beer'.

Glasse was brought up in the gentrified Northumberland household of her father, Isaac Allgood, who had been a Writer in the East India Company. After her husband died she worked as a dressmaker in London but had money problems and was forced to sell the copyright of her book before spending time in Marshalsea debtors' prison. By the time of the 1770 edition, published the year Glasse died, it had been spiced up to include a recipe *To Make a Currey the Indian Way*. It called for turmeric, ginger and pepper 'beat very fine', while mace and cloves were added to the 'pellow' rice. Indian food only became hot when chillies were discovered in the Americas.

Curry powder, a variant of the instant mix of roasted and ground spices, herbs and roots that has helped make dishes such as chicken tikka masala become national favourites, arrived in London around 1780. That is the date of the earliest curry powder advertisement held in the archives of the British Museum. It was placed in *The Morning Herald and Daily Advertiser* by Sorlie's Perfumery Warehouse of 23 Piccadilly. Addressed to 'Persons of Rank, firepower to all Nabobs, and Servants', it claimed that it had been brought from the East Indies not by the Company but by Daniel Solander, the botanist employed by the British Museum's natural history department who had made his name as the first Swede to circumnavigate the globe when he accompanied Captain James Cook on his first voyage of 1768. *"The most celebrated East India dishes and most sumptuous sauces are made from this powder,"* the advertisement ran. *"It is exceeding pleasant and healthful – renders the stomach active. In digestion – the blood naturally free in circulation – the mind vigorous, and contributes most of any food to an increase of the human race."*

It was a century after Glasse's book had appeared that the first curry house opened in Britain. A plaque just inside the glass door of the luxury apartments at 34 George Street, behind the Wallace Collection off Oxford Street, shows the site of the Hindoostane Coffee House that started business in 1810. It was run by Dean Mahomed, who had made a name for himself with *The Travels of Dean Mahomed: An Eighteenth-Century Journey through India,* published ten years after his arrival in London. He came from Patna in Bengal, and when his father, who was in the Indian army, died, Dean joined up, aged eleven, and was under the care of a Captain Godfrey Baker. In 1782 they both resigned and went to Cork, where Dean learned English and married the daughter of a wealthy Catholic family. After the publication of his book he came to London where he found employment with Basil Cochrane, sixth son of a Scottish earl, who had joined the East Indian civil service and amassed a fortune supplying British ships in Madras. Cochrane had a house in Portman Square where he had installed a public steam bath, and here Dean introduced *shampoo*, from the Hindi *champi* for body massage. Cochrane then set Dean up in his curry house nearby to serve dishes *"dressed with curry powder, rice, cayenne and the best spices of*

26

Arabia". Bamboo furniture and Chinese paintings added to the atmosphere, and hookahs with Oriental herbs were available in a smoking room.

But London was not ready for an Indian restaurant. Those who might have been able to afford to eat out preferred to stay with their cooks at home, and it closed within a couple of years. Dean then moved to Brighton where he opened his own baths and reinvented himself as a former East India Company surgeon, adding the title of Sake (sheik). The Prince Regent was so impressed that he installed vapour baths in the Moghul-style Royal Pavilion designed for him by John Nash, and after he was crowned George IV, he made Sake Dean Mahomed 'Shampooing Surgeon to the King'.

In the ensuing Victorian days of the Raj, spices became increasingly available. Curry ingredients and chutney became store-cupboard staples, kedgeree (from Kijari, near Calcutta, an anchorage for large East Indiamen) awaited in the silver salver on the Edwardian breakfast sideboard, and there was mulligatawny soup at the end of the day. Today, of course, Indian food in all its regional diversity is a British staple. Modern as well as traditional, it blends two nations' palates with such popular dishes as 'Roga josh shepherd's pie', the creation of Vivek Singh, the Bengali-born chef and patron of the Cinnamon Club. Around the white-clothed tables of his restaurant in the book-lined  Grade II former Westminster Library parliamentarians sit down with today's company men to snap their popadoms, dish the dhal and set the world to rights.

SILK, SATIN, COTTON, RAGS

There are two places that Londoners especially like to mention to show their knowledge of the city. One is Sir John Soane's Museum in Lincoln's Inn Fields, the other is Dennis Severs' House in Spitalfields.

Sir John Soane was an investor in the East India Company, and its cargoes helped to furnish his Oriental collection. He also loved to drink its tea, which he offered to 1,000 guests who visited his home over three days in March 1825 to see his newly acquired sarcophagus of Egyptian King Seti I, for which the obsessive collector and architect of the Bank of England had just paid £2,000. There, in the first-floor dining room, visitors partook of the East India Company's finest blends among sumptuous furnishings that included gorgeous yellow silk curtains that still look vibrant on the candlelit evenings held once a month at the house-museum.

The ability to pick up and reflect light, to make it shimmer and dance, is just one of the remarkable qualities that have made silk highly sought after for

thousands of years. It was one of the principal early cargoes of the East India Company, which by the mid-18th century had become the global behemoth of the textile trade, accounting for sixty percent of its sales. The company's activities impacted enormously on London's cloth manufactures, particularly the silk weavers of Spitalfields who occasionally had cause to attack the Company, although they may not have been able to survive and flourish without it.

The streets of Spitalfields, on the opposite, east side the City from Lincoln's Inn, contain the best-preserved quarter of early Georgian terraces in London. These tall houses are handsomely porticoed, shuttered and panelled, rising to the 'lights', glazed attics running the width of the buildings under which weavers' looms would clatter, and where immigrant Huguenot weavers would keep bird traps for snaring cock linnets and other song-birds that would brighten their working hours.

It was one of these houses that attracted the American artist Dennis Severs to East London in 1979. Just as obsessive as Soane, if less well funded, he spent the last twenty years of his life turning ten panelled rooms of No.18 Folgate Street into an atmospheric museum that was as near as possible to how it would have seemed to somebody entering the original silk-weaver's home. Gaslit and scattered with the detritus of daily living, it presents the most convincing step back in time to be found in the city.

The off-stage characters that Severs' fertile imagination summoned to inhabit his house were the Gervais family who, he decided, had arrived here in 1729, anglicised their name to Jervis and remained until 1914. They would have been among many thousands of Huguenots who brought their skills from France and made Spitalfields a centre for the textile trade. Protestant Huguenots had been persecuted under Louis XIV, the Sun King who built the Palace of Versailles. This pinnacle of European regal splendour required the products of the country's most skilful craftspeople, and during his reign new silk patterns were ordered twice a year for the court, becoming the basis of the modern biannual French fashion shows. Production was mainly in the south of the country, where the mulberry trees on which silkworms flourished are still in evidence, as are a few of the tall towers used to unravel the yards of spun filaments of the *Bombyx mori*, the silkworm cocoon.

One of the major centres of production was Lyon, where in 1801 Joseph Marie Jacquard devised a loom described by some as 'the world's first computer' because it relied on a punctured paper scroll to programme the pattern. Such a pattern could take three months of uncompensated time to create. Visitors to Lyon today can see an original Jacquard loom in action at the Atelier-Maison des Canuts. There are six professional craftspeople still working on Jacquard looms in the city, and in recent years they have produced silk fabric for the Yellow Room at the White House, for Buckingham Palace and for the Palace of Versailles. Silk wall hangings and curtains for the refurbishment of the Sun King's palace, completed in 2013, kept one of these craftspeople occupied at her loom for twenty-two years. It cost a small fortune.

Since its discovery in China in the middle of the third millennium BC, and kept secret until cocoons were supposedly stolen by two monks acting for the sixth-century Byzantine emperor Justinian, silk has been pure textile gold. Yet its weavers, often deafened and made blind by their work, have not always been appreciated. In 1831 the Lyon silk workers, called *canuts*, caused what is regarded as one of the first labour strikes, but these were not the first revolts by silk workers. The masters of Spitalfields may have had houses built in the handsome style of the ones they had left behind, but the French, English and Irish weavers sweating away in their garrets and garden sheds had to doss down in nearby slum tennemants.

Riots aimed at the East India Company occurred on a number of occasions when imports of finished textiles were seen as a threat to weavers and to tens of thousands of dependent workers in London, including dyers, drapers and finishers. In January 1697 when a Bill to curb imports of finished silk goods was put before parliament, some 4–5,000 weavers' wives marched on the House of Lords, before heading to East India House where the outer doors were broken down. Two months later the weavers' anger was taken out on the Company's Deputy Governor and representative in parliament, George Bohun, who opposed the Bill. A Tory MP, Bohun had been living in Wood Street, off Cheapside, where a Land Securities development now stands, before inheriting from his younger brother property in Spitalfields, where he took up residence and gained a licence to hold a market three days a week on the Artillery Ground, now Spitalfields Market. A second son with no university education, Bohun had long been in trade and, though he was rich, not all his investments had been successful. He had, for example, lost money when the Blackwall-built *Modena*, a sixty-gun, three-tier, 800-ton East Indiaman, went down in a hurricane in March 1692 on a homeward journey from India. None of the 150 crew members survived, though for some fifteen years afterwards Bohun and his fellow investors in the voyage, including former Company chairman Sir Thomas Grantham, fought claims in the London courts for sailors' back wages from the families of the drowned.

Armed with iron bars, pickaxes and other make-do weapons, the mob on that night in March 1697 was rebuffed by Bohun's household staff sufficiently robustly to ensure the family was unharmed until no fewer than seven companies of militia came to the rescue. Two protesters were killed as shots were fired. A few days later a reported 3,000 of them failed in their attempts to assault Wanstead House in Essex, the palatial home of one of the Company's most prominent figures, Sir Josiah Child.

For some decades textile imports had been gathering pace, and by the mid-1680s cotton and silk 'pieces', which were the width of a loom and ten to twenty yards long, accounted for more than eighty percent of the Company's trade. It could compete with silk still coming overland on the Silk Road from China, which was imported either raw from the Ottoman empire or as thread spun mainly in Italy. But it still was not cheap. A race therefore began to find a way of producing the raw material here, of cultivating mulberry trees to nourish the silk worms that produced the thread. In his enthusiasm for the idea, James I even tried to force the Virginia Company in America to swap its tobacco plants for mulberry trees, and it is intriguing to speculate what might have happened had he been successful. In London he had four acres of land on the north side of what is now

Buckingham Palace set aside for a Mulberry Garden. A single tree behind the Hyde Park Gate Lodge claims to have been part of the garden, but it is clearly not old enough, though a 200-year-old tree survives in the garden of Buckingham Palace where in the year 2000 some thirty species were added, with the result that the Queen now has the official national collection of mulberries. King James also sent a directive to the Lord Lieutenant of every English county to instruct them to urge landowners to start planting 10,000 imported trees.

Mulberry Walk in Chelsea is the only sign of another failure, the Raw Silk Company, started in 1718 by the enterprising John Appletree. He assured 1,000 investors that his patented method of silk farming was bound to succeed, and 2,000 trees were planted in the walled Chelsea Park. Five years later a sample of satin made in Chelsea was apparently approved by the Princess of Wales and described as "very rich and beautiful", but despite such valiant efforts, silk was never successfully farmed in Britain, possibly because black mulberries (*Morus nigra*), with a sweet fruit, were planted instead of the white ones that are to the silk worms' taste.

Raw silk continued to be imported under the East India Company's monopoly but the increasing volume of imported printed textiles threatened native printers and dyers, and when the Company was given free trading rights in Bengal in 1716, the floodgates opened. Within three years imports of printed and dyed silk and calico goods trebled. Reaction from English workers was dramatic. In the ensuing 'calico crisis' some 4,000 Spitalfields weavers and their supporters roamed the city attacking any woman wearing calicoes, *"sousing them with inks, aqua fortis* [nitric acid] *and other fluids"*. Female servants, perhaps for the first time able to afford something cheap and cheerful, were dubbed 'calico madams', suggesting they had ideas above their station, and were particular targets of these attacks.

In response, the government passed a Bill that prohibited the use and wearing of *"all printed, stained or dyed"* calicoes and silks. But a taste for Indian and Chinese style had been planted, and there was no going back. At first copied and then originated, Spitalfields designs developed and new ones appeared every season. There is a blue plaque on the house in Princelet Street where one of the leading designers, Anna Maria Garthwaite, lived and worked from 1728, the year before the Jervis family arrived in nearby Folgate Street. She was admired for her knowledge of production methods, and the thousand or so designs for damascs and brocades that she produced, as well as hundreds of watercolours, are in the collection of the Victoria and Albert Museum.

Paris and the French Court still dictated fashion, even during the Seven Years War with France. In 1757 Louis Philippe Boitard, a London-based French engraver, published a satirical scene of fashionable Londoners eagerly viewing cargoes of French goods being unloaded beside the Tower of London. That same year Robert Clive took Bengal from the French at the Battle of Plassey: from here on, Indian muslins, silks, calicoes and chintzes would be available in abundance. To keep manufacturers happy, and to deny Asian industry an export market, the Company was still forbidden to import finished goods. In a further protectionist move, the introduction of powered looms in India was forbidden.

The industrial revolution, however, proved the undoing of the Spitalfields weavers, who could not compete with the new cheap products that began to be churned out by mills powered first by water, then steam, across the Pennines, through Lancashire, Yorkshire, and Scotland. Shortly after the East India Company was dissolved, a treaty was signed with France, allowing French silks to be freely imported.

The textile connections continued when Jews escaping pogroms in Russia and Europe settled in Spitalfields near their point of disembarcation by the Tower, and making it a centre of London's rag trade. In the late 20th century their place was taken by Asians, mostly Bengalis whose ancestors had supplied the East India trade. Names of streets around Brick Lane, Petticoat Lane and Wentworth Street, in  what is now known as 'Banglatown', are written in Bengali, the language of Bengal. There are still large numbers of textile importers and fashion designers here, and weekend markets are popular.

Although there is no sign of its name, this is one of the most visible legacies of the Honourable East India Company in London.

INDIGO

Artists' Colourmen L Cornelissen & Son, 105 Great Russell Street, is one of the most attractive shops in London, and what it doesn't know about colour is not worth knowing. One look in the window is enough to make the passing pedestrian want to stop and step inside, and once inside they will be carried away by an array of materials in mahogany cases, of more colours than were ever in a rainbow, of pigments, oil paints, watercolours, gouache, pastels and acrylics in tubes and blocks and jars displayed on custom-made shelves and neatly packed in numbered drawers. This is the artist's apothecary.

The East India Company was on the eve of its demise when the shop opened in 1855, not here in Holborn but in Covent Garden from where it took both its shopfront and interior when it moved half a mile north in 1977. It has served artists from Walter Sickert and Aubrey Beardsley to Damien Hirst and Tracey Emin, dedicated painters who know how to pound coloured pigments into a liquid that can be applied by pallet knife, sponge or brush. When the shop opened, the world had yet to discover synthetic pigments, but London had already been brightened by the East India Company's cargoes. The cheerful prints of the Indian calicoes they brought were in contrast to the dull English woollen garments the Company had attempted in vain to trade in the East. A number of indigenous plants were responsible for the bright patterns of *chintz*, a Sanskrit word used to describe silk or cotton textiles. A Hindu word, *bandana*, was adopted by East Indiamen sailors who tied these cheerful pieces round their heads to keep their dank locks from their faces.

Southern Asians were masters in the complex process of dyeing and there were many new colours for the Company to discover and exploit. Among the most striking were red madder, India yellow and indigo. The madder plant was found in the calcium-rich seashell shores of southern India. India yellow, a pigment favoured by JMW Turner, was for many years believed to have been made by the urine of cows nurtured by mango swamps. Indigo had been sought since Babylonian times and could be used in creating every shade of blue as well as greens and purples. It doesn't need mordants to bind it to a yarn, and it is colour fast, but it was hard to obtain, and it was expensive.

Among a dozen blue pigments in large jars on Cornelissen's shelves, the darkest by far is indigo. It is almost black. A seven-gram sample jar costs around five pounds and the pigments can be bought on-line. For artists, blue is of prime importance, and from Renaissance times European artists found its richest hue by grinding lapis lazuli, a mineral mined in Afghanistan, into ultramarine. This was the rich colour reserved for church paintings, for the robes of the Virgin Mary, and the clothes of kings. It is also the colour of the Hindu Krishna.

In Europe, blue cloth was dyed with woad, *Isatis*

tinctoria, a member of the mustard family, which has none of the depth and radiance of *Indigofera tinctoria*, a low bush and one of around three hundred varieties of indigo. The name derives from *indikon*, the word that the ancient Greeks gave it simply because it came from India where it is called *nil*. In its first decades of trading, it was the Company's most valuable commodity. A trading monopoly would turn blue into gold.

The main growing area in Asia was in the Sindh, in modern Pakistan, and neighbouring Gujarat in North India, particularly around Agra. Portugal had been the primary European provider of indigo until the British took over Bombay in 1661. The plant was not confined to India. *Indigofera arrecta* was the main variety grown in West Africa, introduced by Arab traders on slave plantations. As blue cloth was a sign of wealth, dyeing was a major industry, still in evidence in the gorgeous colours of robes worn in Nigeria and Gambia, and by the Tuaregs, the Sahara's 'blue people', whose skin is often stained by their indigo robes. A love of blue garments meant that there was still a hungry market for the indigo that the Company could readily obtain in India.

The Atlantic was beyond the Company's sphere of influence and although *Indigofera suffructiosa* existed in Central and South America, it was the French colonialists who introduced *Indigofera tinctoria* to the Caribbean, notably Haiti, where it grew to equal the economic importance of sugar. Africans, particularly Yorubas, who were familiar with growing indigo and dyeing with it, were sought by slave traders to work the Caribbean and North American plantations.

Eliza Lucas Pinckney is credited with starting the 18th-century indigo bonanza in North America. In 1740, at the age of eighteen, she planted indigo seeds on the family estate in South Carolina. Her father, Colonel George Lucas, had sent the seeds from Antigua, where he had been summoned to take up the post of British Governor of the island, leaving his daughter to look after the farm. It took several seasons before the crop became productive and the success allowed her to spread seeds among neighbouring plantations. At the outbreak of the War of Independence, with Colonel Lucas dead and Eliza siding with the rebels, indigo accounted for thirty-five percent of the colony's income. Benjamin Franklin sailed to France shortly after the start of the war taking a consignment of indigo provided by Congress, the only acceptable currency to hand, to pay for establishing America's first embassy in Paris.

The years of hostility lost America a market for indigo in Britain, though there was a new outlet for the blue uniforms of the Continental troops, who wanted to be seen in contrast to British redcoats. In the meantime in Britain there was an increase in demand for coloured textiles generated by the industrial revolution, and the Company redoubled its efforts to extract indigo from India and ensure Bengal remained the world's largest producer. Plantations were taken over and dye factories were set up to turn the plants into cakes or bricks that would be transported in barrels. A model of an indigo factory in Bengal

with a hundred workers, which was made for the 1886 Colonial and Indian exhibition, is on display at The Royal Botanical Gardens in Kew. But the treatment of peasant farmers in Bengal, who were forced to plant indigo in place of food crops and were driven into debt by planter overlords, is an episode that the Company cannot have been proud of. The Indigo Revolt of 1859 occurred after the Company had folded but grievances went back half a century.

The colour blue became an advertisement for the East India Company through its naval officers and Blue Coat private army. Master mariners had blue frock coats, with white waistcoats and breeches that could be shown off with a pinch of indigo when washed, an Indian trick that made whites whiter than white. An attempt by the Court of Directors to introduce crimson waistcoats was rejected, while linen was soon dyed buff, thus no doubt camouflaging any spilled tea.

In adopting a uniform, the Company was following the Royal Navy's example. Anxious to overturn its reputation as a national institution for society's dregs, the Navy had come up with the idea of a uniform in 1748, emulating the manly fashions of court dress. Commissioned officers at first wore tailcoats and full-bottom wigs, and the market for indigo greatly increased when all seamen were required to wear sailor suits. London's new police force set off on their beats in top hats and blue tailcoats, too, and young men were given tails at charitable Bluecoat Schools. Veteran mariners who retired to Wren's Naval Hospital in Greenwich wore blue jackets, as opposed to the scarlet ones worn by inmates of Wren's twin Royal Hospital in Chelsea. Pensioners' cabins have been re-created in the Greenwich Visitor Centre near the tea clipper *Cutty Sark*, and on pegs beside them are blue coats, plus tricorn hats, to try on for a souvenir photograph.

Today, blue is recognised as the world's favourite colour, and the legacy of the indigo trade is unmissable. On any London street, on any tube journey, half the pedestrians and passengers may be wearing blue jeans. Made of cotton twill, the material used by Levi Straus was woven from a warp of two or more indigo-dyed yarns and an undyed weft, so their surface was bluer than the reverse. As the dye does not penetrate cotton yarn, over time it rubs off, allowing these utilitarian trousers to fade well. So many textiles and garments have Asian names, it is surprising that there is no Indian word for blue jeans, which derives from the French town of Nîmes, where denim was made, and Genoa (Gènes), where it was turned into trousers. There was one coarse cotton cloth from Bombay, however, that has not translated, from the Hindi *dungri*.

Dungarees, jeans, service uniforms, blue-collar workers may not immediately conjure the East India Company's name, but there is no doubt that it played a part in turning the world's wardrobe blue.

TEA

Fortnum and Mason is London's high temple of tea. Here are to be found more than eighty blends, irresistibly packaged, assiduously prepared and elegantly served. Above the hush of the emporium's deeply carpeted halls, tea caddies, gift packs, fine china, teapots, infusers, strainers and cozies are parcelled up by saleswomen in turquoise cravats and men in raven-black frock coats. In the Diamond Jubilee Tea Salon, the royal-warrant holders maintain the benchmark for English afternoon tea. Waistcoated waiters arrive with the full Monty of finger sandwiches, scones, cakes and fragrant brews in wafer-thin porcelain, and a brief lesson in what's what is offered by 'tearistas' who help to choose from black, white, green and yellow blends.

Tea made Fortnum's famous, and it made the East India Company famous, too. It was the Company that created the plantations in India to help make it the world's most popular beverage, and despite the encroachments of coffee shops, tea remains Britain's favourite hot drink, with around 165 million cups or mugs drunk every day. Before Fortnum's, however, came Twinings in the Strand, which started

life as Tom's. It was one of scores of coffee houses that had been popular meeting places in London for more than fifty years before green tea arrived from China and a century after the Company's maiden voyage to the east. A Turkey and East India merchant, the original Tom was Thomas d'Aeth, who sold his business to Thomas Twining, a protégé and tea enthusiast, in 1707. Twining's speciality teas appealed particularly to women customers from nearby wealthy houses who could afford their high prices, and he was soon selling more dry tea than cuppas. In spite of Thomas Twining's commercial success, it was not until the 1840s that afternoon tea was made fashionable. It is said that Anna Russell, Duchess of Bedford, instigated the event to bridge the hunger – and perhaps conversation – gap between lunch and dinner. Unwelcome, and indeed unwilling to visit coffee houses that were rank with men and tobacco, women especially appreciated tea taken in the pleasure gardens of Georgian London.

The Twinings became rich. A miniature portrait of Richard, the founder's grandson and a director of the East India Company, was among twenty-five painted by John Smart that went on show at the Philip Mould Gallery in Dover Street in 2014. Smart spent ten years in India painting miniature portraits of Company men, and some of them, like Twining's, were set in an oval frame of some five dozen diamonds. The firm stayed in the family hands until the 1960s, when it was sold to Associated British Foods who acquired another prestigious tea company, Jacksons of Piccadilly, which had been in business since 1815 and claims to have invented the Earl Grey blend. In a further spin of the globe, Twinings closed its packing plant on South Shields in 2011, and relocated to Poland – and China. But the shop on the Strand is still there. All manner of teas can be

sampled and individually blended, traditional black and red metal caddies can be bought and there is a small display from the company's history.

Tea had been growing in China for thousands of years before it reached western Europe, through the Netherlands and Portugal's early trading posts in Canton and Macau. A letter containing the first known recorded use of the word 'tea' in the annals of the Company's history was sent to a Mr Eaton, the agent in Macau, in 1615. It was written by a Mr R.L. Wickham, a Company merchant operating in Hirado, Japan, where the Company had been for two years, and where the Dutch and Portuguese were already established. The letter asked Mr Eaton to send "*a pot of the best chaw*".

It was not until thirty-five years later that the Company shipped the first tea samples to London, from Canton. Initially tea was deemed a medicine, an infusion with a variety of promised cures, and it was extremely expensive. The sociable epicurean Samuel Pepys tried it in 1660, a decade after the first coffee house had opened in London. Then secretary of the Navy Board in Seething Lane, Pepys had been discussing with colleagues the affairs of Spain and

France, when he "*did send for a Cupp of Tee (a China drink) of which I never drank before*".

The following year, a couple named Harris became caretakers at East India House, and Mrs Harris became the Company's first tea lady. She would brew for the meetings of Directors whose discussions at that moment were greatly exercised by the newly restored Stuart monarchy. Charles II had returned from nine years' exile in France and the Netherlands where, thanks to the Dutch East India Company bringing the first large shipments of tea to Europe, he was *au fait* with the Chinese infusion. On his restoration, the city of Amsterdam presented him with a royal yacht built by the Dutch East India Company. It was Britain's first royal yacht and, with a narrow draught and large sail area, it was a precursor of the Thames sailing barge.

Everyone was anxious to find favour with the king, and he was happy to encourage them. Hedging their bets, the Directors had already supplied the king with loans during his exile, and now the whole city needed his favours. Years of austerity during the republican interregnum had come to an end, and the guilds splashed out on a procession that marked the monarch's triumphant return. Andrew Riccard, the Company's Governor whose statue and monument in medieval St Olave's church in Hart Street eclipses that of Pepys opposite, instructed the Directors to "*shew their loyal affection*" by giving the king 100 ounces of silver plate. A new royal charter favourable to the Company swiftly followed.

A solution to Charles's immediate financial demands was his marriage to Catherine of Braganza. Not only would she arrive with a generous dowry from her father, João IV, but she would also bring Portuguese overseas territories, including seven islands of Bombay on the west coast of India. In return for many favours to come, Charles allowed the Company to rent Bombay for £10 a year. It would become the Company's main station in India under a Presidency that encompassed Gujarat as well as Aden in the Yemen and the Sindh Province of Pakistan. Today, as Mumbai, it is the most populous city in the country.

Among the sacks of sugar, spices and other bounty from the Portuguese empire that accompanied Catherine on her pre-nuptial voyage from Lisbon was a consignment of tea. Nobody on board the British naval ship knew how to brew the beverage that she asked for to calm her queasiness, and she was instead offered a glass of beer. They would soon learn. When, shortly afterwards, the first East Indiaman arrived in London with a shipment of tea, the Company naturally presented a large sample to the king. With such influence at court, it was not long before the fashionable were taking tea.

Tea was initially drunk from porcelain bowls, following the custom in China and Japan where tea was whisked in hot water in a formal ceremony. Bowls were imported along with the dried leaves that were carried in containers shaped like ginger jars. Holding just over a pound of tea, equivalent of one Chinese *catty*, the measurement of weight apparently gave its name to the tea caddy. Larger, more elaborate caddies, some lacquered and inlaid with mother-of-pearl, were meant for dining-room display. Though often used as ballast, Ming porcelain brought in a vogue for 'China ware' that proved hard to replicate: the Meissen works in Germany had the first success in Europe, in 1705. It has been suggested that the habit of putting milk in tea originated in early attempts at making bone china, as boiling water poured directly onto less successful pieces would cause them to crack. Sugar, another fashionable commodity, was added to the more astringent black teas of India when plantations in the Caribbean dramatically reduced the price.

Catherine had been on the throne for seventeen years when the first recorded auction took place at East India House, conducted by Company brokers. At the subsequent quarterly 'candle sales' of China tea, the auctioneer's hammer came down as each mark on a burning candle was reached. It has been estimated that a single cargo of tea would be worth around £200 million today, and at the height of business some 1,200,000 pounds of tea might be sold in one day. The habit took a while to filter down to ordinary people, but in time it would become cheap enough for tea and toast to replace the British breakfast of beer and beef.

The Company was a victim of its own success. A tipping point came when increasing demand hit the barrier of high taxes, and tea became the smugglers' item of choice to such an extent that the East India Company's fortunes were threatened. Since the Company was judged too big to fail, in May 1773 the Tea Act was passed to help with its mounting debts. The Act granted a monopoly on tea sales to the colonies, though it was not allowed to export to them directly. Duty paid on importing tea to London would be waived if it was then exported to America, where taxes were still due. Paying taxes but denied a vote was not something that the inhabitants of the New World could stand. Three American ships, *Beaver*, *Dartmouth* and *Eleanor* had sailed to London with cargoes of whale oil, and for the return journey to Boston picked up consignments of the East India Company's China tea. On the night of December 16, shortly after they had docked, 342 chests were ceremoniously dumped into Boston Harbor's Griffins Wharf by patriots dressed as Mohawk braves. "Perhaps salt water and tea will mix tonight," said ship owner John Rowe, apparently approving an

attack on one of his own ships. Today there is an annual re-enactment of the Boston Tea Party that sparked the American Revolution. Visitors pay 25 dollars a head to climb aboard replicas of the *Eleanor* and the *Beaver* to experience Boston's No.1 tourist attraction. So it might be said that America is at last profiting from the East India Company.

Smuggling became less attractive after 1784 when the government attempted to discourage this lucrative activity by dropping the tax on tea from 119 percent to 12.5 percent. This helped to ensure London as the world centre for the tea trade. In the General Court Room at East India House brokers would put in their bids in increasingly rowdy exchanges, described in the early 19th century as appearing to be "*a mere arena in which the comparative strength of the lungs of a portion of his Majesty's subjects are to be tried. No one could for an instant suspect the real nature of the business for which the assemblage was congregated.*"

This bear pit was an international market; two-thirds of the world's tea consumption passed through the auction house. There were also many English buyers, and tea found its way around the country onto the shelves of the increasing numbers of local shops where new exotic imports such as tobacco, sugar and pepper were for the first time being sold. (In Spain grocers were – and some still are – called *ultramarinos*, meaning their products came from 'beyond the sea'.) Tinplate canisters were decorated with Chinese designs to look Oriental, and varieties were put side by side on shelves of mahogany, the exotic timber imported from Asia as well as South America.

The rise of an independent USA, which could freely trade with China, was compounded by the loss of the Company's monopoly rights in Asia, and after 1834 it began to look for safer ground to source its tea. China had never much wanted English goods, and the Company had for decades been forced to buy tea with silver until it began trading opium, grown in India and exported through Calcutta, which it endeavoured to force on the Chinese population. It became imperative to find another source of tea.

Robert Fortune was the well-named man the Company chose for searching out the finest of many hundreds of varieties of *Camellia sinensis* for the Company to plant outside China. As superintendent of the Hothouse Department at the Horticultural Society's garden at Chiswick, the Scottish plant-hunter had been sent on a collecting mission to China in 1843. There he learned Mandarin, wore his hair in a *queue* – bald on top with a ponytail – and came to public attention by writing an account of his three years in the country. He was the ideal candidate for the East India Company to hire for a second

journey to China to collect samples of tea that could be established in India. So after serving for two years as curator of Chelsea Physic Garden, he duly set off once more.

The high plateau of Assam in northern India was chosen for the initial plantations, but in the end these failed, a disaster thoroughly retrieved when it was discovered by a team from the Calcutta Botanic Garden that there was actually a local Indian tea plant, with a slightly larger leaf, and it was this that in the end made Assam the world's largest tea producing area, a title now held by Kenya. Unlike green China tea, the leaves of *bohea*, or black, tea were left in the open to oxidise.This darkened them and ensured they held their flavour on the journey to London, which from bush to teapot could take up to two years. Chests were of differing sizes, depending on their origin, and they were lined with lead to keep the tea fresh. The first Indian harvest arrived in the London sale rooms in 1839, on the eve of the Opium Wars with China. By then the Company's monopoly had already ended, and trade patterns had begun to change. Auctions were being held in producing countries and large companies started dealing direct with suppliers.

A dancing academy in Change Alley on the south side of the Royal Exchange was hired for the first free trade tea, which had arrived in 1834, and as volumes increased, bolstered by the cargoes of the fabulous tea clippers, larger premises were sought. For nearly half a century, from 1834, two storeys of the warehouse that is now home to the Museum of London in Docklands were used as tea warehouses, and this excellent museum tells some of the story of the tea trade. Another was in Creechurch Street, off Leadenhall Street, now occupied by the Old Tea Warehouse pub with little to show what it once was.

By the late 19th and early 20th century auctions were being held four times a week in the London Commercial Salerooms, then in Plantation House, both in what came to be called 'the Street of Tea', Mincing Lane. The buildings have since been pulled down and replaced by the extensive Plantation Place office block. At the last auction, held on June 29, 1998 in a rented room in London's Chamber of Commerce, just 400 tons of tea were auctioned.

America, meanwhile, had become a nation of coffee drinkers. Thanks to the Boston Tea Party, tea was deemed anti-American, the drink of traitors. But in recent years there have been signs of a renewed taste for the colonial brew. Until Starbucks took off in Seattle in 1971, American coffee had something in common with tea – it tended to be thin and watery, and was too often left to stew. To begin with, Starbucks advertised its wares as 'coffee, tea and spice', and offered twenty-seven different types of loose-leaf tea in what could have been an advertisement for the East India Company two centuries earlier. Then, in 2012, the company paid $620m for Teavana, an American tea-shop chain, opening its first tea-only outlet in New York the following year, and later announcing an ambition to open a thousand tea outlets, introducing a special Oprah Chai Tea for the television personality's favourite drink. The company estimated the value of the global tea market to be $90 billion, and it was after a slice of it.

In London, tea has been undergoing something of a revival, too. Most surprisingly, the East India Company name has been resurrected by a company selling teas and own-brand 'fine foods and luxury gifts'. Based in Mayfair's Conduit Street, and with a number of outlets around the city, it has a 'tea library' of more than 100 varieties includes Directors Blend Green Tea, which honours the Company's bosses, and Staunton Earl Grey Tea, which takes its name from Sir George Staunton, the traveller and diplomat who is credited with inspiring the Earl Grey flavour after noticing Chinese bitter oranges growing alongside tea bushes. In England, with no Chinese plant available, the rind of bergamot oranges was added to black tea to produce a similar taste, and the resulting brew was named after the incumbent prime minister.

Long since out of use, the East India Company name had been acquired in the 1980s from the Treasury by a group of English businessmen who were also granted use of the Company's coat of arms. In a fitting reversal, it then came into the hands of a Mumbai-born businessman, Sanjiv Mehta, and after some £12 million was spent on developing the business, the store opened in 2010 on Indian Independence Day, August 15. A canny businessman who cut his teeth in post-Soviet Russia, Mehta comes from a wealthy family of diamond traders.

Following the launch of EIC Fine Foods, he was interviewed for the journal *Caravan* by a former classmate, Salil

Tripathi, who had sat with him as a schoolboy, learning about the history of the Company in India. Tripathi wrote how, after explaining that he thought his whole business life had led to this moment, Mehta *"...then gets up, excited, to show me a box holding the Company's original Merchant's Mark, known as the 'chop', which was dipped in ink and stamped on the goods of The East India Company from the 17th century. He cradled the box in his arms, as if it were an infant. 'Imagine – the East India Company. It is mine!'"*

DIAMONDS

Every year around three million visitors tour the Tower of London. It's the city's most-visited paid-for attraction and it is not cheap but it provides a good day out, offering an atmospheric stroll through the past thousand years of English history. It is also a lesson on how politics can be as dangerous as navigating the high seas. Among many famous and infamous figures incarcerated in the Tower was Sir Thomas Smythe, the first Governor of the East India Company, for apparent conspiracy in the Earl of Essex's attempted plot against Elizabeth I. Innocent, he was soon freed and later returned to be knighted here by James I. His tale comes a long way down the list of names remembered in the former royal palace.

A highlight of any visit is the Crown Jewels. The gold, silver and platinum crowns sparkling with all manner of precious stones are immediately recognisable symbols of the monarch's wealth and power. The Imperial Crown of India, worn only once, by George V at the Delhi Durbar, has more

than 6,000 diamonds. But the most fabulous single stone in this unmatched collection of headwear, is the Koh-i-Noor diamond which the East India Company acquired by force of arms. Until 1725, when discoveries were made in Brazil, India was the world's sole source of diamonds, and the fabulous mines of Golconda were a by-word for wealth. Long-since exhausted, these were in an area from around Hyderabad to the east coast above Madras, today's Chennai, where the Kollur mine on the Krishna river produced some of the most spectacular diamonds, including the Koh-i-Noor. The Company had access to rubies, too, which were found in Ceylon and Burma.

When customs duties on precious stones were abolished by Parliament in 1732 it was because *"This kingdom has now become the great mart for diamonds and other precious stones and jewels, from whence most foreign countries are supplied."* London remains a global distribution centre for rough diamonds, and the name of Hatton Garden, where more than a thousand jewellers, craftsmen and designers continue to work, has become synonymous with the trade.

The earliest surviving written evidence of the Koh-i-Noor is in the 15th-century memoirs of Babur, the first Mogul ruler of India. Over the following 400 years, the diamond passed through a number of hands before becoming the property of the Sikh rulers of the Punjab. When the East India Company army under James Andrew Broun-Ramsay, 1st Marquess of Dalhousie, won control of the Punjab in 1849, the diamond was an explicit part of the punitive peace treaty.

Dalhousie was the son of a Peninsular War general, and had been President of the Board of Trade before being appointed Governor-General of India by the Board of Directors. At thirty-three, he was the youngest to hold the post and he carried out his duties entirely as he thought fit. He was a pivotal figure, arriving at the end of the Company's life – causing its death, according to some – and the birth of Britain's Indian Empire. In command of the East India Army, he had ambitions to expand the Company's control, proposing to annexe any state whose prince died without a male heir. On arrival he became almost immediately involved in the Second Anglo-Sikh War, which led to the Company taking control of the Punjab. The great prize of the campaign was the Koh-i-Noor, which was written into the concluding Treaty of Lahore. Deemed spoils of war, it was to be "*surrendered by the Maharaja of Lahore to the Queen of England*".

Dalhousie spoke for the Company, but he acted unilaterally, and when the Court of Directors complained that he had not arranged formally to acquire the diamond for the Company, so that the Company could be seen to give the stone to the Queen, Dalhousie replied that he did not want the diamond to be seen as a gift, "*which is always a favour by any joint-stock company*"; it was better it passed directly from Maharajah to Queen "*with no favour inferred*". Dalhousie himself took it from Lahore to Bombay to find a ship. It was "*sewn and double sewn*" into a belt fastened by a chain round his neck and not removed until he reached his destination many days later. "*My stars! What a relief to get rid of it!*" he wrote when he finally handed it over to a Company ship at the port.

At Portsmouth, it was given to two Company officers who conveyed it to East India House in London and from there the Deputy Director took it to the Queen. She would later receive it officially from

Duleep Singh, the deposed 13-year-old successor to the principality, who was brought to England to formally hand it over.

The diamond made headlines. It was of one of the curiosities of the Great Exhibition in Hyde Park in 1851, displayed in a golden cage in the India Court, the Company's showcase. Other precious stones acquired by the Company were on display, including the 352.5-carat Timur Ruby, which had been another prize in the Lahore Treasury. At the end of the Exhibition, mindless of Dalhousie's caveat about 'gifts', the Directors of the Company presented a delighted Queen Victoria with this ruby and a magnificent selection of jewels.

The Koh-i-Noor's public outing was not, however, a complete success. Prince Albert was among many who were disappointed that the diamond was not sufficiently brilliant, and he had it recut. It took more than a month to reduce its weight by around forty percent to 108.93 carats and create an oval shape with thirty-three facets. It was then set in a tiara with some 2,000 lesser diamonds, and five years later made the starring stone in a regal circlet of jewels. Meanwhile the Timur Ruby was set in a necklace by the royal jewellers, Garrard, in such a way that it could be replaced when necessary by the Koh-i-Noor.

Rumours of bad luck attached to the ill-gotten diamond, fuelled by the publication of Wilkie Collins' *The Moonstone*, were ignored by Victoria, and though it was said that it would blight any man, it was thought it could not possibly adversely affect a woman. Perhaps as a result, it has never been a part of a male monarch's regalia. In 1911 it was set in a coronation crown containing nothing but diamonds for Queen Mary. For Elizabeth Bowes-Lyon, Consort of George VI and the future Queen Mother, it was set in a Maltese Cross at the front of a platinum crown based on Queen Victoria's regal circlet. She wore it once, for her coronation, and its second public outing was in 2002 when it was placed on her coffin for her three-day lying in state in Westminster Hall.

In France, one of the most celebrated jewels is the Regent Diamond. Now in the Louvre, it was last  utilised in a Greek diadem made for the Empress Eugenie for the World's Fair in Paris, which followed shortly after the Great Exhibition. It had adorned the crowns of French kings since 1722, and Marie Antoinette wore it in a headpiece. In 2014 this was fancifully re-created with a suitable three-masted ship by the artist and historian George S. Stuart, and shown at the 'Diamonds are Forever' exhibition in the Ventura County Museum in California.

In England, where the Regent was known as the Pitt Diamond, it helped to create a political dynasty. Thomas Pitt was a maverick adventurer from Dorset. By the age of twenty-one he was pursuing a career as an 'interloper', someone who traded in the East without the Company's consent. His activities came to the attention of the Directors in London in 1675 and they sent orders to Madras to have him arrested, describing him as "*a fellow of haughty, huffying, dazing tempers*". Pitt slipped away, and continued trading in India and Persia for the next half dozen years before returning to London and facing the charges. He accepted a £400 fine with equanimity and was by now wealthy enough to buy his way into parliament. He purchased estates at Old Sarum in Wiltshire, one of the notorious 'rotten boroughs' that returned an MP although there was, rather importantly, nobody actually living there, and hadn't been since the castle and community had abandoned the settlement in the 14th century.

Pitt's knowledge of business in the East was generally acknowledged, and having acquired a degree of respectability, he was approached by the Company to become President of Fort St George and subsequently Governor of Madras, a position he held for a dozen years. On arrival, he made great changes to the governing body, including the licensing of his oldest son, Robert, to act as a 'free merchant' at the Fort.

Diamonds were a regular part of the trade in Madras, and Pitt sent them back to London by way of remittances. The diamond that was brought to him in December 1701, however, was much too good for the Company. It weighed 410 carats and was the largest Pitt had ever seen. The man offering it to him was a well known local diamond dealer named Jamchund, and if he hadn't stolen it, others certainly had. It came from the Parteal mine in Golconda where it had been purloined by a bonded labourer who cut his leg and then wrapped the wound in a bandage that contained the diamond. Escaping to the coast, the story has it, he met an English sea captain, who either bought the diamond or stole it after dispensing with the labourer, but nothing more is known of this part of the story. On reaching Madras the sea captain apparently sold the diamond to Jamchund who, after two months of negotiations, sold it to Pitt.

It was Robert who was entrusted to bring it to England, and on reaching London his father had it cut into a cushion shape, which reduced it to 136 carats. The £6,000 bill for the cutting was covered by the 'cleavage' and dust produced in the process. Through the mediation of the Scottish economist John Law, Louis XV's Controller General of Finance, it was sold to the Duke of Orléans, heir to the French throne, and Thomas himself took it to Calais in 1715, accompanied by Robert.

Thomas Pitt used his riches to buy Swallowfield Park near Reading in Berkshire. This extensive, Grade II listed manor has now been turned into twenty-seven apartments, and residents can use the period grand hall, reception rooms and library, as well as the twenty-five acre garden where two rivers flow.

Pitt consolidated his position in politics, continuing to offer advice to the Company. On his death at Swallowfields in 1726, Robert stepped into the parliamentary seat of Old Sarum, as did his son William, who became prime minister and 1st Earl of Chatham. The earl's son, William Pitt the Younger, was also returned to Parliament from the phantom Wiltshire seat to become Britain's youngest prime minister at the age of twenty-four. One of his major successes was the India Act of 1784, passed during his first year in office, which set up a Board of Control to stamp out corruption in the East India Company and put it under a degree of government supervision.

Pitt is commemorated by a statue by Francis Chantry on a pedestal in Hanover Square, his head aloof in the canopy of London plane trees. The

Company had always tried to ensure there were members in Parliament to speak on its behalf, but it was not until 1832, twenty-four years after Pitt's death, that the Reform Bill was introduced to sweep away 'rotten boroughs' such as Old Sarum. When the statue was erected some months earlier, Reform Bill agitators saw it as a symbol of corruption and attempted to pull it down. Yet it might not have been there at all had it not been for his great-grandfather, 'Diamond' Pitt.

FAUNA AND FLORA

Just after midnight on the morning of February 3, 2014, triplet tiger cubs were born at London Zoo. It was a milestone moment, recorded for the first time by a hidden camera. Their mother Melati and their father Jae Jae were both born in captivity, and because Sumatran tiger numbers in the wild are estimated to be as low as 300, the event was hailed as a great success for the Zoological Society of London's breeding programme of rare animals.

London Zoo in the twenty-first century is not as wild as it once was. English Heritage has listed the 20th-century animal houses, designed by Berthold Lubetkin and Sir Hugh Casson, and banished the elephants and rhinos to the suburban savannah of Whipsnade where they were joined by the lions while their kingdom was undergoing a massive rebuild. Architectural tours mingle with flocks of schoolchildren. No wonder that tigers, symbols of India, have been getting top billing.

Sir Stamford Raffles, Governor of Java and Sumatra, founder of Singapore and one of the East India Company's most celebrated employees, was a driving force behind the Zoological Society of London, and its first president. On the northern edge of Regent's Park in land gifted by George IV, the society was intended not for public entertainment but for serious study, and for the first few years its zoo was open only to members.

Raffles had joined the Company as a Writer at the age of fourteen. His father was an impecunious Yorkshire sea captain who at sixteen had set sail for the West Indies where he came in contact with the sugar plantations and slave trade. Born on board his father's ship off Jamaica, Thomas Stamford grew up in Walworth's East Street in South London, dropping the name Thomas to avoid confusion with a cousin who became a noted preacher in Spitalfields. In 1804, aged twenty-four, fair-haired, self-tutored and thoroughly sociable, he was sent on an East Indiaman to the island trading post of Penang in Malaya, where he would start his first menagerie. Within seven years he was successfully ousting the Dutch to bring Java under the Company's control. At his residence in Bogor, he took on and expanded the botanical garden, which is still in existence, and in 1819 he purchased Singapore island on the tip of the Malayan peninsula for the Company, creating the botanical garden there, too.

Raffles remained in South-East Asia for twenty years as Governor first of Java and then Sumatra, in an attempt to consolidate the Company's monopoly over this string of fertile islands that slip down beside the Malayan peninsula and swing eastwards to the Moluccas Spice Islands. He learnt to speak the language and wrote the *History of Java*,

glowingly described by one contemporary as "*an ornament to oriental literature*", in which he laid out the ethos of his administration, vowing to rule "*not only without fear, but without reproach*". Supported in his work by the liberal Governor-General Lord Minto, he took an interest in the people and the local culture. Affected, perhaps, by his father's first-hand accounts of the slave trade, he is cited as ensuring slavery was not practised on Company estates, and he withdrew licences for gambling and cockfighting.

Raffles' chief pleasure and ambition lay in the search for botanic and zoological specimens. He collected menageries wherever he went, and enjoyed taming animals himself, to the extent of dressing up a pair of orangutans that were sent from Borneo by the Sultan of Pontianak.

After Java was handed back to the Netherlands, he returned to England for eighteen months, arriving with thirty tons of baggage. It included many ethnic curiosities, now in the Raffles Collection, which the British Museum acquired after India House was closed. Divided between the Ethnography and Oriental Antiquities departments are ornate gamalan instruments, Javanese puppets, metalwork and figure carvings. Hidden away in the museum's north London depository are instruments of torture found by Raffles that had been used by the Dutch on the local population.

His last post was as Governor-General at Fort Marlborough in Bencoolen in Sumatra where he and his wife, Sophia. lived, and shortly after his arrival he established a trading post in Singapore. It was not his particular desire to return to England again, but he was about to be put out of a job by the Anglo-Dutch Treaty that ceded to the Dutch the island of

Sumatra in return for the Company's continued rights over Singapore. Four of their children had died by this time and their only surviving child, Ella, had already been sent back to London,  but Raffles' nephew and the young son of a colleague were to accompany them on their last journey home.

Raffles' vast library of South-East Asian flora and flora illustrations would confirm his reputation among London's leading men of science. The ship was crammed with exotic plants as well as animals destined for his new London zoo. Correspondence and research material from naturalist friends Joseph Arnold and William Jack were added to his own invaluable papers. Silver plate and Sophia's not insubstantial jewellery was also safely stowed. The vessel was named *Fame*, which would be appropriate as they made their triumphant way up the Thames to the East India Docks, where Londoners' natural curiosity for the new and unusual would be thoroughly satisfied.

At around twenty-past eight on the evening of February 2, 1824, however, some fifty miles out of Bencoolen, the ship caught fire. A steward carrying a naked candle had gone to draw off brandy from a barrel in a cabin beneath the couple's berth where Sophia had just climbed into bed and had "*nothing but a wrapper, no shoes and no stockings*", while the children were snatched from their bunks as the flames licked at their sides. In less than half an hour, as passengers and crew filled two boats and began to row back towards Bencoolen, the ship started to go down but it was not until midnight that fire met the cargo of saltpetre. The spectacular explosion seemed to light up the whole world and Raffles could only look on, appalled.

"*[I] lost all my collection in natural history,*" he wrote, "*all my splendid collection of drawings, upward of two thousand in number, – with all the valuable papers and notes to my friends, Arnold and Jack; and, to conclude, I will merely notice that… there was scarce an animal, bird, beast, or fish, or interesting plant, which we had not on board: a living tapir, a new species of tiger, splendid pheasants &c, domesticated for the voyage; we were, in short, in this respect, the perfect Noah's Ark.*"

It was something of a miracle, the press reported, that no lives were lost, animals not counting as lives. It would be easy to fantasise a different outcome in which Sir Stamford was cast alone on a boat with his new species of tiger, a prequel to Yann Martel's *Life of Pi*. What this 'new species' of tiger was is unclear. It may have been one of two Indonesian species that have now died out, from Java and Bali, or it may have been a Sumatran tiger. What is certain is that in 1902 the last tiger in Singapore was cornered in Raffles Hotel. Shot as it lurked beneath a table in the billiard room, it is part of the history of this glamorous establishment where Rudyard Kipling and Somerset Maugham stayed, and where tales are told over gin slings in the Long Bar.

Raffles Ark Redrawn was published in 2009. His collection had not been resurrected from the depths of the Indian Ocean; the 126 illustrations in this new book had been made for Raffles by local artists in the time between the sinking of the *Fame* and his final departure for England ten weeks later. These became part of the Raffles Family Collection that the British Museum added to their Raffles Collection in 2007, and were then compiled in a single volume by Henry J. Noltie of the Royal Botanic Garden Edinburgh. It included birds, flowers, fruit, herbs and spices, with information on their culinary and medicinal use. Most spectacular of the plants is the

Rafflesia arnoldii, a parasite that produces the world's largest flower, up to a yard across and weighing some twenty-four pounds. A putrefying smell that attracts insects has given it the nickname of the 'corpse flower' and it is one of two dozen species named after Sir Stamford. Following his return to London, he ordered a wax model of it to be made, and this is now in a glass case in the Royal Botanical Gardens. A catalogue in the archives at Kew also shows that Raffles had returned from Sumatra in the autumn of 1824 with a 'clouded leopard', *Felis nebulosa*, which was then sometimes referred to as a 'clouded tiger', and perhaps this was similar to the one that went down with the *Fame*.

The loss of the *Fame* did not stop Raffles from immediately setting about his task of establishing the Zoological Society, though he faced the usual charges of embezzlement aimed at so many administrators by the Court of Directors. He had a house in Berners Street, off Oxford Street, and four months later he purchased High Wood, a farm near Hendon with an eight-bedroom house, now Grade II listed, near his friend, the abolitionist William Wilberforce. Here, on July 5, 1826, on the eve of his forty-fifth birthday and three months after taking up the presidency of the Society, he was found by Sophia at the bottom of the spiral stairs. Death was caused by some kind of stroke.

The Company charged his estate with £10,000 for his debts. His subsequent high reputation was largely due to Sophia, who lived at High Wood for a further thirty-two years, and to her hagiography, *Memoir of the Life and Public Services of Sir Thomas Stamford Raffles, FRS &c &c*, the etceteras implying an ennui of honours. A statue by Chantry was installed in Westminster Abbey where it sits on a plinth with a 155-word inscription that has no mention of the East India Company, but commends him for having *"secured to the British flag the maritime superiority of the eastern seas"*.

Raffles' grave in the attractive and ancient church of St Mary's in Hendon was, however, unmarked. The vicar, Theodor Williams, who had been born in Jamaica and still had connections with the sugar plantations, was so opposed to Raffles' stand on the sons of Ham and their freedom from slavery that he refused to allow any memorial. In fact it was only in 1914, with the reconstruction of the church, that Raffles' body was identified and a proper granite slab was laid by the altar steps. Barely legible now, the modest memorial says simply that he was Lieut-Governor of Java and founder of Singapore.

Two dominant statues of Sir Stamford still stand in Singapore. The first is outside Victoria Hall, which commemorated the centenary of his arrival, and the second, a white polymarble statue copied from this original, was set up on the Singapore River in 1972 at Raffles Landing in the business district, opposite the spot where he is supposed to have first set foot on the island. Like the memorials in London, neither of the statues in Singapore has any mention of the East India Company, to which he owed his loyalty, his riches and his fame.

The work that Raffles had begun with the Zoological Society of London moved on apace, and its zoo opened in Regent's Park two years after his death. George IV, the eponymous former Prince Regent who gave the Society a royal charter, was a fan of the fashionable and exotic, and had made Raffles a Knight of the British Empire. Not only had Nash designed for him the Royal Pavilion in Brighton, with tented roofs, domes and minarets, but he also received the first giraffe to be seen in Britain, a gift from the Pasha of Egypt, for his Windsor menagerie the year after Raffles died.

British monarchs had filled menageries since the 13th century, as any visitor to the Tower of London soon discovers. But they also liked them near their homes. James I kept camels, crocodiles and an elephant in St James's Palace gardens, and when Charles II opened the gardens as a park, the public could admire the birds in the aviary in what is now Birdcage Walk. He expected avian gifts, and much else, from every

← BIRDCAGE WALK SW1
CITY OF WESTMINSTER

Company ship returning from the East, and exotic waterbirds remain a feature of St James's Park.

The death of George IV in 1830 marked the transfer of royal beasts to the new London Zoo. Among the animals brought over from the Tower was a pair of lions that Colonel Watson of the East India Army had presented to the king in 1823. He had caught the cubs in Bengal after bagging their parents, and the male was named George. The naturalist Edward T. Bennet published a booklet on the Tower menagerie in which he wrote about George's arrival. "*On the voyage he was remarkably tame, allowing the sailors to play with him, and appearing to take much pleasure in their caresses. On being placed in his present den he was rather sulky for a few days, but seems now to have covered his good temper, and be perfectly reconciled to his condition.*" The tigress was similarly sulky on first arrival, but she too soon settled down to her urban environment.

Exotic beasts and plants had been arriving by the shipload during the eighteenth century, and it had become imperative that they were categorised and given a name that would be recognisable in any country in the Western world. Latin was therefore the language chosen by Carl Linnaeus, the originator of the system named after him. *Homo sapiens* is of his devising; *Panthera tigris sumatrae*, and *Panthera leo persica* are the taxonomic names for the Sumatra tiger and Asian lion. Scores of animals and plants are named after Company men. *Rafflesia arnoldii*, for example, was named after Sir Stamford and Joseph Arnold, who had accompanied him on the expedition that collected the plant, though there is no place for the name of Sophia, who was also on the trip and completed Arnold's drawing of the flower following his sudden demise.

As a doctor, Carl Linnaeus was interested in plants used in medicine, and when George Clifford, a director of the Dutch East India Company, asked him to organise the plant collections at his famous private zoo and botanical garden at Hartekamp near Haarlem, he jumped at the opportunity, and it was there that he began devising his system. He first came to London in 1736 at the age of twenty-nine to see Sir John Soane at the Chelsea Physic Garden, and he was subsequently the leading light of Uppsala University. Botanists of that time were trained in medicine, many at the famous faculty in Edinburgh. But the Company's first official Naturalist and Botanist was Johann Gerhard Koenig who was from the Duchy of Courland, now in Latvia. A pupil of Linnaeus', he was working in India when he was appointed, and the celebrated botanical gardens that he went on to establish in Calcutta led him to be regarded by some as the founder of modern botany in India. Before his appointment in 1778, he had been in Madras where he became friends with William Roxburgh, a young Company surgeon from Ayrshire, whose eminence in the botanic world would more than match Koenig's. The botanical expeditions they enjoyed together continued after Roxburgh was sent as a Company surgeon to the hill town of Samalkot, several hundred miles north of Madras, where he created experimental gardens, growing various spices as well as plants for cultivating cochineal beetles and silkworms, and he employing Indian artists to make scientific drawings.

Drawings were as important as specimens to the Board of Directors in London, who relied on the knowledge of Joseph Banks, the first director of the Royal Botanic Gardens at Kew. Made famous as the botanist on Captain James Cook's first voyage of 1768–71, he was a towering figure of enlightened eighteenth-century London. Five years after his return from the voyage he acquired a large house in Soho Square where 20th Century Fox now has its London headquarters. Like his country estate in Leicestershire, the house was soon cluttered with the chaos of enquiry and discovery, and visitors had to be careful where they were treading. With a tea house in the basement and philosophical breakfasts, this was a place of the meeting of restless minds. A large library took up the back of the house and Banks was assisted by Daniel Solander, a fellow student of Koenig's from Uppsala. It was at this house in Soho that the Linnaean Society first met.

At the time of Carl Linnaeus's death in 1778, Banks was getting on in life, and so when he was offered the Swedish naturalist's entire collection of plants, manuscripts and books to purchase, he turned the offer down. However, he suggested to a wealthy medical student and protégé, James Edward Smith, that a sure way to success would be to buy the lot, which he did, and the Society was set up by Smith soon afterwards.

The Linnean Society is now one of the Courtyard Societies that occupy Burlington House, Piccadilly, and his statue, bearing the inscription 'illustrious

foreigner' is among figures arranged in niches around the central square of this campus for the arts and sciences. The Society's home is on the left under the entrance arch and its elegant library, which can be visited by appointment, is looked down on by portraits of Smith and Linnaeus. Occasional tours take in the Linneaus collection, which has been immaculately conserved in a custom-made bomb-proof strong room in the basement. All Linneaus's library is here, including folio editions of his seminal *Systema naturae* of 1735. The herbarium

of some 4,000 pressed plants is shelved in paper wallets lined with linen to prevent acid attack, and there are drawers full of remarkably preserved specimens, from fish and beetles to startlingly blue butterflies that have kept their colour.

Through co-operation between these botanists and societies, plants were identified and trialled not just across South-East Asia, but across the world. The Company sourced quinine and other drugs, discovered foods and flavourings, dyes and lacquers, and attempted to spread their production. Banks also set out directives as to how plants should be illustrated, how they should be described and how they should be transported.

Until 1829 when Dr Nathaniel Bagshaw Ward, a doctor from Wapping, inadvertently discovered plants' ability to survive in a sealed container, creating the Wardian Case or what today would be called a terrarium, money often had to be found as a bribe to prevent the specimens' on-board neglect. Occasionally a Chinese gardener would accompany the plants, to return home the following season, but generally East Indiamen captains and crews were given instructions about their care. Salt had to be wiped from their leaves and only rain water should be used to feed them.

Every spring there is a Camellia Show in the 300-foot conservatory at Chiswick House in West London, which was restored to its original 1813 glory in 2010. These specimens, relations of the

tea plants, came from China, and during restoration the history of many of the plants was traced, particularly through East Indiamen logs. The date of their arrival and the name of the ship's captain and purchaser were tracked down. Two species are even named after the Company's captains: the deep pink *C. reticulata 'Captain Rawes'* and the white *C. japonica 'Welbankiana'*. The Duke of Devonshire, owner of Chiswick House, also acquired orchids through the Company for his collection at Chatsworth House in Derbyshire.

Roxburgh had been sending Banks specimens and illustrations from Madras and the Coromandel Coast for a couple of years when Koenig died from dysentery. Roxburgh attended him during his illness, and subsequently took his place, sending Koenig's material to Banks who concluded that he had "*repaid the East India Company a thousand-fold over in matters of investment, by the discovery of drugs and dyeing materials fit for the European market*".

As Superintendent of the Calcutta Botanic Garden, Roxburgh continued to commission illustrations of plants that would become the *Flora Indica*, an encyclopaedic collection of 2,542 drawings and 3,379 foolscap pages of descriptive material. A duplicate set sent to the Company was donated to Kew where there are also illustrations for Roxburgh's *Plants of the Coromandel Coast*, from his time in Madras. More than three hundred of them have the EIC stamp on the back. Roxburgh had intended to publish his *Flora Indica* but ill health had twice forced him home and he died in

Edinburgh in 1815. A few years later his manuscript text was published but the illustrations were too expensive to reproduce.

The great wealth of material that accumulated at Kew remained largely disorganised until after the Second World War when Robert Sealy, a botanist on the staff, began looking into it. By 1956 he was able to provide an alphabetical list of all the plants described by Roxburgh, and this can now be accessed on Kew's website. All the originals are still in Calcutta Botanical Gardens' 1960s building that stands in a hundred hectares of garden, as the British writer Victoria Finlay discovered when searching for 'the last indigo plant' for her 2002 book, *Colour*. Arriving unannounced, she found herself sifting through one of the thirty-five volumes of Roxburgh's 2,600 illustrations. Volume Eight contained twenty-three varieties of *Indigofera*, and as she opened it, "*the leather cover fell off in my hand... The colours had not faded much in two centuries, although sadly the paper had long ago started its journey towards disintegration in the tropical humidity.*"

Roxburgh was followed by Nathaniel Wallich, who had been born in Copenhagen and gone to India as resident doctor to the Danish East India Company. Stationed at Serampore fifteen miles upriver from Calcutta, he was, through the vagaries of European wars, briefly a prisoner of the British. It was under Wallich that the Calcutta Botanic Garden blossomed as a pleasure garden with a staff of three hundred. Wallich sent plant collectors all over Asia, and he travelled extensively himself. One of his missions was in 1835 to the newly conquered territory of Assam where *Camellia sinensis* had been reported growing, and it was Wallich's party who had made the discovery of Assam tea. Under a newly formed Tea Committee, the Board of Directors in Leadenhall Street had sent him a directive asking him to try to see the plant growing for himself. He was joined by a colleague and a Dr John McLeland who, typically, was employed as both geologist and surgeon and who later wrote: "*We were fortunate enough to find it both in flower and fruit; its growth is tall and slender... Their leaves were all large, of a very dark green, and varying from four to eight inches in length*." And so the tea industry in India began.

Wallich's incumbency marked the high point of the botanical garden, and he sent 8,000 specimens back to the Directors in East India House. When the Company disbanded half a dozen years after his death, botanic material was taken from its basement. Much of it was not labelled, pressed leaves and flowers were in shreds, if not dust, and it took a dozen years for the dedicated staff at Kew to catalogue what was salvageable. Today the Wallich Herbarium is the name usually given to the The Herbarium of the Honourable East India Company, the largest herbarium at Kew, containing material on 9,149 species, and many of the the 200,000 illustrations held in the Botanic Gardens' collections were made for Company men. Any of them can be seen by appointment, but the only time they are on public display is in special exhibitions.

Kew remains preeminent in international botanical research, and in 2013, following advances in DNA, it re-categorised the taxonomy of some of its seven million plants, which the Linnaeus system had attributed to what is now seen as the wrong species or group, though it wasn't too far out. Meanwhile behind the scenes the search goes on for cures for cancer, tuberculosis, Parkinson's and other diseases, but the global hub established by Joseph Banks and his successors is still there to be seen around the 300-acre grounds, from William Chambers' Chinese Pagoda to the many plants from Asia, including the camellias that colour a large patch in spring. Seven species of palm are named *Wallichia*, and in the steamy Palm House there is an atmosphere of those tropical climates that the Company men knew. The black pepper bush is luxuriant, the nutmeg,  tumeric, and tamarind plants, too, and while the banyan tree twists upwards, in the marine basement the upside-down jellyfish show what lurked in the beds of mango swamps.

With such a vast collection of plants and seeds and a wealth of scientific knowledge, in the summer of 2015 Kew was able to put on a special exhibition titled 'Full of Spice' and celebrating "*the mystical yet brutal world of the spice trade*", in which plants "*once worth their weight in gold, were so valuable they changed the world*".

COMPANY MEN

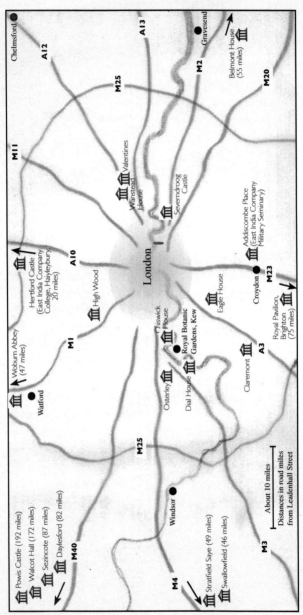

Chelmsford

A12

A13

Gravesend

Belmont House
(55 miles)

M2

M20

M25

M11

Valentines

Severndroog Castle

Wanstead House

Addiscombe Place
(East India Company
Military Seminary)

Hertford Castle
(East India Company
College, Haileybury,
20 miles)

A10

Eagle House

Croydon

M23

High Wood

London

Woburn Abbey
(47 miles)

Chiswick House

Royal Botanic
Gardens, Kew

Royal Pavilion,
Brighton
(75 miles)

M1

Osterley

Claremont

A3

Dial House

Watford

Powis Castle (192 miles)

Walcot Hall (172 miles)

Sezincote (87 miles)

Daylesford (82 miles)

M25

About 10 miles

Distances in road miles
from Leadenhall Street

M40

Windsor

Stratfield Saye (49 miles)

Swallowfield (46 miles)

M4

M3

78

RICH & FAMOUS

There is no statue in the City of London either to Robert Clive or to Warren Hastings, the East India Company's two most famous figures. Clive defeated the Nawab of Bengal and his French allies in 1757 at the Battle of Plassey, which brought Bengal under Company control, while Hastings, appointed first Governor-General in 1773, consolidated the Company's hold over India. They are remembered for their trials as much as for their triumphs. Addicted to laudanum and suffering from gallstones, Clive is said to have committed suicide in his Berkeley Square home at the age of forty-nine. His corruption trial, in which he was accused of acquiring £234,000 to the dishonour and detriment of the state, had not helped. On Hastings, too, an impeachment and seven-year trial for corruption and mismanagement took a toll, although he was finally exonerated.

Yet by the time India was made part of Queen Victoria's domains, both had become woven into the unimpeachable fabric of Empire. Forgiven their faults, they were no longer seen as corrupt Company men, lining their pockets and protecting the interests of a City institution and its shareholders, but as national heroes, founders of a civilising empire that stretched across one fifth of the world on which the sun would never set. Boys were given 'Clive' as a first name to ensure his fame lived on. Victoria, Empress of India, settled into her ivory throne after East India House in Leadenhall Street had been swept away. Taking its place was the India Office in Whitehall, a government department that was fully accountable to Parliament. A magnificent Italianate building was designed for just that purpose. Looking across St James's Park to Buckingham Palace, it would be part of a new complex centred on three quadrangles that included both the Foreign and Colonial offices, all three today combined into one Foreign Office. Opposite, on the south side, is the Treasury, and the passage in between is Charles Street, which leads to Clive Steps, a grand flight descending to St James's

Park. At the top stands an imposing statue of Robert, first Baron Clive of Plassey, sculpted by John Tweed, 'the Empire Sculptor'. It was erected in 1912 to celebrate the coronation in New Delhi of George V and Queen Mary as Emperor of India and Empress Consort. With a sword at his side and bronze reliefs of his successes around the plinth, it confirmed Clive as Britain's great empire builder whose actions would one day bring the monarchy the subcontinent's crown. The reliefs show the 1751 siege of Arcot, the 1765 Grant of Bengal from the Rajah and a lonely, pensive figure in a mango grove on the Ganges' banks on the eve of the Battle of Plassey. But nowhere is there any mention of Clive's employers, the East India Company.

Tweed also carved Clive's simple memorial tablet in the south aisle of Westminster Abbey, which has the barest inscription: '1725 Clive 1774'. Until then, Clive had not been included in the ranks of Company men commemorated and buried in the nation's most magnificent historic building and one of London's most expensive tourist attractions.

Clive's career had been mercurial. The oldest of thirteen children and an unruly boy, he had been taken on by the Company as a Writer and sent to Madras, entering the military shortly afterwards. His successes at Arcot and Trichinopoly and, most decisively at Plassey, drove the French from India.

After Clive had returned to England, the 1760 *Annual Register*, edited by Edmund Burke, reckoned his fortune to be £1.2 million in cash, bills and jewels, while his wife's 'casket of jewels' was estimated to be worth £200,000. "*So that he may, with propriety, be said to be the richest subject in all three kingdoms,*" the journal concluded. Clive may have been involved in many underhand dealings that helped to make his fortune, but when brought before a parliamentary committee to answer charges of peculation and forgery, he defended himself robustly, claiming that when he had entered Moorshidabad, the newly acquired capital of Bengal, he "*walked through vaults thrown open to me alone, piled on either hand with gold and jewels... By God, Mr Chairman, at this moment I stand astonished at my own moderation.*"

The East India Company made him fantastically rich, and he was regarded as a classic *nabob*, a word taken from the Hindi *naawab*, meaning a landowner or ruler. In England it was used pejoratively to describe a man who had gone to India and made his fortune, to return to a life that was far above his station. The East India Company may have called itself 'Honourable', but it was still 'trade'. A comedy at the Haymarket in 1772, written by Samuel Foote and titled *The Nabob*, helped to spread the word. Its protagonist was a Company man, Sir Matthew Mite, who on his return to England from India sought the hand of Sir John and Lady Oldham's daughter, an outlandish request made palatable by Sir Matthew's promise to pay off the family debts.

The Nabob Rumbled is a cartoon by James Gillray, now in the National Portrait Gallery's collection, showing Thomas Rumbold vomiting a shower of guineas into a chamber-pot. Rumbold was Clive's aide-de-camp at Plassey and subsequently Governor of Madras, in which position he acquired sufficient funds, estimated at £600,000, to buy two parliamentary seats, at New Shoreham and Shaftesbury. He lost both when it was shown he had paid huge bribes in exchange for votes, and he was eventually fired from his directorship of the Company.

As for Clive, there were stories of how, in London, he ordered a hundred shirts at a time to

be delivered to his handsome house at 45 Berkeley Square. William Chambers spent four years from 1763 modelling the interior. Born in Sweden, Chambers had been employed by the Swedish East India Company and had made three trips to China, inspiring him to design the Chinese pagoda at Kew. But the grand columned hall with a top-lit staircase overlooked by a second-floor gallery, decorated with fine plasterwork and chimney pieces that he designed for Clive was more in tune with

prevailing Palladian fashion than Eastern exoticism, and it suggests that Clive wanted to be seen not as a nabob with foreign ideas, but on a level with Europe's aristocracy. Now Grade I listed, the house was in the Clive family hands until his great grandson died in 1891, and is now owned by a property development company. It is one of the finest surviving 18th-century interiors in London. Members of Annabel's and the Clermont Club next door at No.44 will have had a glimpse of the kind of grandeur of Clive's home.

As a result of his greatest victory Clive was made Baron Clive of Plassey, County Clare, and in seeking a position among the landed gentry bought estates in Ireland as well as Clarement House in Surrey (described in the next chapter), which he proceeded to demolish and rebuild. It did little to enhance his reputation. The historian Thomas Babington Macaulay, who drafted the Indian penal code and introduced English into Indian schools, was not impressed: "*The peasantry of Surrey looked with mysterious horror on the stately house which was rising at Claremont, and whispered that the great wicked Lord had ordered the walls to be made so thick in order to keep out the devil, who would one day carry him away bodily.*"

The devil carried him away from No.45 Berkeley Square on the night of November 22, 1774. The next day the historian and man of letters Horace Walpole, who had a house at No.11 and had been scathing about the nabobs, had no wish to speak ill of the dead when he wrote: "*The nation had another great loss last night — Lord Clive went off suddenly. He had been sent for to town by some of his Indian friends — and died... Lord H. has just been here, and told me the manner of Lord Clive's death. Whatever had happened it had flung him into convulsions, to which he was very subject. Dr Fothergill gave him, as he had done on like occasions, a dose of laudanum; but the pain was so violent, that he asked for a second dose. Dr Fothergill said 'if he took another, he would be dead in an hour'. The moment Fothergill was gone, he swallowed another, for another, it seems, stood by him, and he is dead."*

Warren Hastings had not long been appointed Governor-General of Bengal when he heard the news of Robert Clive's death. Hastings had been at Plassey, and Clive, seven years his senior, appreciated his talents. Both believed that the Presidencies should be combined beneath an overall authority, the new post that Hastings had just taken up.

Though born in modest circumstances in Oxfordshire, Hastings had, unlike Clive, some pedigree. His family estate of Daylesford in the Cotswolds had been in the possession of his ancestors since the reign of Henry II but had been lost when fortunes waned during the Civil War. One day he would buy it back. He went to Westminster School and joined the East India Company at seventeen, sailing for Calcutta the same year. Rising through the Company, he put an emphasis on languages, learning to speak Bengali, Farsi and Urdu, and understanding local customs. Despite measures to drive out corruption, or perhaps because of them, his own record came under heavy questioning. He certainly enjoyed a good living in India with his second wife, Mariana Anne Chapuset. She had been married to Baron Christoph Carl Adam von Imhoff, and had come to London under the patronage of Juliana Schwellenberg, a childhood friend who had been made Mistress of the Robes to Charlotte of

Mecklenburg-Strelitz, the wife of George III. The Baron, a demobbed officer from the Württemberg army, was trying to make a living as a portrait painter. Having little luck in London, he had been advised to go to India, so he obtained a cadetship in the Company's Madras army and in 1769 he and Mariana boarded the *Duke of Grafton* and headed East. Hastings, then a thirty-seven-year-old widower, was a fellow passenger about to take up a position in Madras, and the on-board romance is said to have blossomed when he fell ill and she attended to him.

Hastings' subsequent marriage to the Baroness was a scandal that only added to his fame. Mariana became a noted *nabobina*, who dressed flamboyantly and loved to wear jewellery. According to the novelist and diarist Fanny Burney, she made everyone at Hastings' subsequent trial, which was something of a social occasion, look underdressed. "*A modest & quiet appearance & demeanour would have been more fitting,*" she wrote.

Not long after the couple had arrived in India the Baron returned to England, having, it is said, been paid off to the tune of £10,000, though his paintings had not been entirely unsuccessful. One of them, *A British Officer of a Madras Sepoy Battalion, Possibly Captain Mathias Calvert (1733–1779), Attended by a Young Sepoy or Servant,* is held by the National Army Museum, and the V&A has a miniature by him. Imhoff was, however, overshadowed by the German painter Johann Zoffany, who sailed for India a couple of months later after his royal commissions in England dried up. He painted many pictures of India and of Company men and their families, including *The Cock Match,* now in the collection of the Tate. Hastings proved a good patron, sitting for portraits and commissioning a picture of himself and Mariana with an Indian servant beneath a tree, and Belvedere House, their mansion at Alipore, Calcutta, in the background. Completed in 1787, the painting is reminiscent of Gainsborough's *Mr and Mrs Andrews* of which Zoffany would have been well aware, and it now hangs in the Victoria Memorial Hall, the gallery of European art in what is now Kolkata, a twelve-hour flight from London.

In the Hall's West Quadrangle is a handsome statue of Hastings, in an academic gown, flanked by a turbanned Muslim reading the Koran, and a Hindu Brahman with a palm manuscript. These had been sculpted by Richard Westmacott and shown at the Royal Academy in 1828 and 1829, but no permanent place was found for them in London, so they were shipped to India and erected at the Victoria Memorial Hall when it opened in 1921.

During his impeachment hearing in Westminster's Great Hall, Hastings lived in Somerset House, the site now occupied by the Marriott London Park Lane. In his lengthy defence, he explained that it was out of affection that he had bought back his family estate, for which he had just paid around £11,000. He estimated that his trial cost him £21,840, but when he was finally exonerated of all charges in 1785 he was compensated by the Company to the tune of £4,000 a year. His reputation subsequently improved, and although he was never knighted or ennobled, he was made a Privy Counsellor. He retired to Daylesford where he remained contentedly for the last years of his life, surrounded by paintings and other souvenirs from India and attempting to introduce cashmere goats and Bhutan cattle, as well as planting the large kitchen garden with lychees and other exotic plants.

Mariana had to pay for the modest memorial tablet placed high on the wall of the north transept in Westminster Abbey, but in a 300-word eulogy she ensured the Company's gratitude should not be overlooked: *"...he restored the affairs of the East India Company, from the deepest distress to the highest prosperity, and rescued their possessions from a combination of the most powerful enemies ever leagued against them...and for his distinguished services he received the thanks of the East India Company, sanctioned by the Board of Control."*

Neither this, nor the memorial to Clive, the two most notable figures of the Honourable East India Company, is a patch on the two aggrandising monuments erected in the Abbey by the Company to Major General Stringer Lawrence and Lieutenant General Sir Eyre Coote, both contemporaries of Clive and, like him, Commanders-in-Chief of the British Forces in India. Stringer Lawrence had encouraged Clive in his career, and their deaths were only a year apart. His monument, just inside the Abbey's West Door, is flanked by two adoring female figures: winged Fame and the Company personified, with flags of India and France beneath her feet. Eyre Coote led a division at the Battle of Plassey, became commander-in-chief four years later, and died in India. His marble sarcophagus beneath Warren Hastings' small tablet rises in an exuberant slab with a palm tree decked about with trophies and flags, his medallion suspended by the figure of Victory. In the opinion of Sydney C. Grier, editor of *The Letters of Warren Hastings to His Wife* (1905): *"Had he [Eyre Coote] lived to return to England, he must in consistency have been included in the accusation [against Hastings]. Since, however, he was dead,* felix opportunitate mortis, *the Directors proceeded to build his sepulchre in the approved style by voting him a monument in Westminster Abbey and a statue at the India House.*"

Also in the North Transept, in what was to become The Statesman's Aisle, is a monumental tribute to General Wolfe who, two years after Clive had taken Bengal, defeated the French on the heights of Quebec, to add Canada to the British Empire. Had Clive, like Wolfe, died in battle, or like Eyre Coote simply expired abroad, he may have had his own great monument in this national pantheon. Yet however much he was ignored by the nation, he could not be ignored by his employers who, despite their reservations about his conduct, had good reason to be grateful to him for bringing them Bengal. At the end of the war with France, his statue was among a triumvirate ordered by the Company for East India House from the Flemish sculptor Peter Scheemakers. Robert Clive, Major-General Stringer Lawrence and Admiral Sir George Pocock, commander of the East Indies forces that backed up Clive's advances, were depicted bareheaded and in Roman dress, a curious fashion of the times.

These three statues now stand in the corridors of power in the Foreign Office, designed by Matthew Digby Wyatt. Surveyor of the East India Company in its last days, Wyatt had worked under Isambard Kingdom Brunel and been Secretary to the Great Exhibition. Now he was employed to create the government's India Office, working alongside George Gilbert Scott, who had been given overall responsibility for the new Foreign Office buildings. At the heart of Wyatt's masterpiece was the Durbar

Court, a three-storey colonnaded yard initially open to the sky, with a marble floor that glistened like the pool of an Indian water garden. Statues of Company men who had served as governors and military commanders in the East were installed in niches around the Court. Paintings, sculptures, furniture, fittings, books and documents were taken by the cartload from the City to the

new Whitehall building before being dispersed to museums, libraries and other institutions. However, a number of items found a home here including an oval painting titled *The East Offering its Riches to Britannia* by Spiridione Roma, from the Revenue Committee Room in Leadenhall Street.

The main meeting room in the new India Office was the first-floor Council Chamber overlooking the Durbar Court and giving a glimpse of what the Directors' Court Room might have looked like. The twelve-foot-high double doors at its entrance are from Leadenhall Street, as is the 1730 fireplace by

the Flemish sculptor Michael Rysbrack with a relief of *Britannia Accepting the Riches of the East*. Too precious to be in daily use, the original table and chairs are in storage, but the chairman's seat, with the Company logo carved in its back, sits in a corner, while a barometer hangs on the wall and a clock shows the time in both London and Delhi.

Warren Hastings is here, too, among the portraits looking down on the table where the Secretary of State for India and his council would hold their meetings until Independence in 1947. The full-length picture shows a mature, balding man, who has lost the romantic air of his youth that comes across in Joshua Reynolds' painting of 1768, when he was in his mid-thirties. Now in the National Portrait Gallery, off Trafalgar Square, it featured in a 2005 exhibition 'Joshua Reynolds: the Creation of Celebrity'. In the painting Hastings wears a *shakulah*, a long silk waistcoat patterned with roses, beneath a blue jacket with gold piping. On the table beside him are books in Persian, the language of the Moghuls of North India, which he had mastered, and his gaze is directed dreamily towards the East.

The National Gallery's East India collection also has *Clive Receiving the Homage of Mir Jaffir after the Battle of Plassey*, an early version of a much larger crowd-pleaser, now lost, painted by Francis Hayman for the Rotunda Gallery in Vauxhall Gardens in 1760. It was one of four paintings commissioned from Hayman to celebrate Britain's triumphs in the Seven Years' War with France.

One further curiosity of the Gallery's collection is a mannequin of Joseph Collett, the Deputy Governor of Sumatra and Governor of Madras. One-foot nine-inches tall, in wig and long red coat with a *shakulah*, sword and a tricorn under his arm, it was made of clay and bamboo by a Canton artist, Amoy Chinqua, in 1716. These small figures were popular souvenirs to ship home, and this one, still in its original rosewood case, was sent by Collett to his daughters, with whom he lived at Hertford Castle for five years until his death in 1725. The castle would later serve as the first home of the East India Company College. Renowned for his bar bills at the Madras 'public table', Collett was twice admonished by the Company for the excessive quantities of expensive claret, Burton ale, Madeira wine, Shiraz, arrack and Goa toddy that had been consumed in his name. *"This is an extravagance that every one of you ought to blush at the thought of,"* the Directors wrote to Fort St George.

Such excess might have been the reality, but it is not something that a Company man would have liked to be conveyed to friends and relations at home. He would have wanted to be regarded as a civilised and civilising individual, and if he could not afford the services of a high-class model maker, he could go for a cheaper, off-the-peg number, like the one in the collection of the V&A. Here is a louche Company servant reclining on a couch in a silk dressing gown, reading some uplifting tract, no doubt in Sanskrit or at the very least in Persian. His head is overlarge, suggesting, perhaps, that bodies were already prepared. One can imagine the model maker touting for business, promising to create, at an absolutely unbeatable price, an excellent likeness to go with a pose most suited to the customer's image of himself as the ideal Company man.

MANY MANSIONS

Robert Clive bought two country estates: Walcot Hall in Shropshire and Claremont House in Esher in Surrey. He had a mile-long lake dug in Walcot's 80,000 acres and gave William Chambers further employment redesigning the mansion and stable block. Clive's son, Edward, added a ballroom to accommodate a large carpet measuring forty-five feet by eighteen feet, which had been given to him when he was Governor of Madras. The carpet stayed in the family hands until after the Second World War when it was bought at auction, according to the Hall's history, by 'two swarthy gentlemen' for the 'government of Azerbaijan'. The house has belonged to the Parish family since 1957, and its gardens are open to the public on two days each spring. It has self-catering accommodation, and the ballroom where the auction was held can be hired.

Clive's other country mansion, Claremont, is now a school, but the thirty-acre gardens, with a turf amphitheatre by a lake where an annual arts festival is held, are run by the National Trust and open to the public. The original house was built by John Vanbrugh, architect of Blenheim Palace, as his own country home, and before Clive's arrival Charles Bridgeman and William Kent had landscaped the gardens. Clive had Vanbrugh's house demolished and hired Lancelot 'Capability' Brown to design his new Palladian mansion and garden, and re-route the Portsmouth road to give the house more seclusion. Brown's future son-in-law, Henry Holland, did much of the interior. This was Holland's first architectural project, and he would go on to redesign the last manifestation of East India House in Leadenhall Street in 1796. Although the building was in fashionable Classical style, the dining room was to have more than a  touch of the East, with plasterwork of camels and elephants. Clive planned large canvases to fill the walls, which he commissioned from Benjamin West. The first of these, *Shah 'Alam, Mughal Emperor (1759–1806) Conveying the Grant of the Dhiwani to Lord Clive*, is a massive fifteen-foot by ten-foot canvas but it was not completed until after Clive's death, and it is now in the care of the British Library.

A thirty-minute train journey from Waterloo, followed by a fifteen minute bus ride, Claremont Landscape Garden is not particularly easy to reach on public transport. The reward is a pleasant garden with little sense of the man who conquered India, as his house is only visible from the garden in winter when there are no leaves on the trees. The National Trust has focused on the house's royal connections, which were established by Victorian times, but Clive does crop up on one of the white benches inscribed

'*A delightful place—*'
Clive of India, 1773

with quotations. His absence is not too surprising as he did not live to see his mansion completed, nor did he live to see his son, Edward, become Governor of Madras and 1st Earl of Powis. The great treasures that Clive had acquired, which he intended for display at Claremont, eventually found a home in Powys, Mid-Wales, not far from where he had been born, the oldest of thirteen children, at Styche Hall near Market Drayton in Shropshire, now converted into apartments. He is buried nearby in St Margaret's, Moreton Say, the church where he had been baptised. His father had been MP for Montgomeryshire, and for the last fourteen years of his life Clive was MP for Shrewsbury, supported by Lord Powis, leader of the Whigs. After Clive's

death, Edward inherited his father's baronetcy and married Lady Henrietta Herbert, heiress to Powis Castle and estate, some twenty miles north of Walcot Hall, providing them with both titles and a secure ancestral home. The minerals that Henrietta collected while the couple were in Madras can be seen in the Museum of Wales.

Their souvenirs were added to the many glittering prizes inherited from Robert Clive, and the remaining pieces of the collection are now in the Clive Museum in Powis Castle's specially designed Hindu-Gothic room, in the care of the National Trust. Among some three hundred items are Robert Clive's chain mail and elephant goad, a gilt and silver Durbar ceremonial dinner set, rose water sprinklers for refreshing guests, spice boxes, betel-leaf caskets and his dazzling gilt and silver huqqa pipe for smoking opium, covered in rubies, emeralds and diamonds. To view the remaining artefacts associated with the East India Company's most famous employee, it is therefore necessary to travel 200 miles from London, to this medieval castle near Welshpool. However, the most astonishing item from the Clive collection is not there. It is 200 miles north of London in the Royal Armouries in Leeds. An almost complete suit of elephant armour, made of thousands of iron plates, the largest of its kind in the world, was the most startling item that Lady Henrietta brought home. It was kept at Powis Castle until 1962 when it was given to the nation along with a number of Clive's other treasures in lieu of death duties for the 4th Earl of Powis, who had left his estate to the National Trust.

There is no museum to Warren Hastings, and his spirit must have long departed Daylesford. He had the house rebuilt in the picturesque Anglo-Indian style by Samuel Pepys Cockerell, a descendent, through his mother, of the famous diarist. Cockerell was architect to the East India Company, and though he had never travelled to India, he went on to build the ideal Indian Moghul-style mansion, Sezincourt House. This Cotswold property had been purchased by his brother, Colonel John Cockerell, on his retirement from Bengal, because he had wanted to be close to Hastings. It was a visit to Sezincourt that inspired the Prince Regent to commission John Nash to design the Royal Pavilion in Brighton in a similar fashion. In 1944 Sezincourt was purchased by the Kleinwort banking family who continue to run the 4,500-acre agricultural estate. The garden was designed by Humphry Repton and its temples, grottoes, waterfalls and canals have caused it to be it likened to the Taj Mahal. The house and garden are open to visitors in summer.

Mariana survived her husband by nineteen years,

and the many luxurious treasures they had acquired in the East were sold off after her death, some of the carved ivory furniture coming to rest in the V&A. The house then went through many hands, including those of the newspaper baron Lord Rothermere, who purchased it in 1947 and entertained there regularly. It was next bought by the art collector Baron Hans Heinrich Thyssen-Bornemisza, who married his Spanish wife, Tita, here, which set him on the road to creating their Madrid museum. The house and park now belong to Lord Bamford of JCB, manufacturers of construction vehicles, who has on occasion loaned

his helicopter to his neighbour, Prince Charles. The gardens open to the public in summer, and Lady Carole Bamford, a keen organic farmer of whom Hastings would undoubtedly have approved, set up the Daylesford organic farm shop on the estate, with outlets in Notting Hill, Pimlico and Marylebone.

Among the prize possessions of Company men's mansions were Persian and Indian carpets, but a carpet was the undoing of Robert Bell of Eagle House in Wimbledon, one of the last surviving Jacobean manors in London. Bell lived in Leadenhall Street and was one of the 215 founders of the East India Company. He had followed in his father's footsteps in the Worshipful Company of Girdlers, and further involvement with the Company helped to make him rich. Not everything he did, it seems, was above board. He first ran into trouble with the Company for attempting to smuggle wine to India on an East Indiaman, but he came really unstuck when he presented the Girdlers with a floral carpet "*seven yards long and three and a half broad, with his own and the Girdlers' arms thereon*" with five shields and Mughal palmates, woven in the royal workshops at Lahore. Accused by the Company of failing to pay for the carpet, he was fined seventy sacks of pepper. Now known as The Bell Carpet, it is a prized possession of the Worshipful Company of Girdlers in Basinghall Avenue, Moorgate.

Bell built his mansion in 1613 on land he had inherited, and an upstairs room was set aside for William Pitt when it was leased by Pitt's cousin, William Grenville. It acquired its eagle, which perches above the central gable, when it was a school, which Lord Nelson and Lady Hamilton visited just before Trafalgar. The blue plaque on its facade ignores these illustrious names and commemorates instead Arthur Schopenhauer, who pursued his philosophical ideas here as a fifteen-year-old schoolboy. In 1988 Eagle House was bought by a Saudi oil magnate, Sheikh Ahmed Zaki Yamani, and for two decades it became a library and research centre for Al-Furqan Islamic Heritage Foundation. It was here, during the summers of 2004 and 2005 that Nick Robins wrote his enlightening study the East India Company, *The Corporation that Changed the World*. After Eagle House's extensive gardens had been bought by developers, it went in sale on 2011 for £8.5 million, to be converted into flats.

A few miles farther west, in Twickenham, is the house that Thomas Twining built. Two buildings had previously stood on the site, and the year 1726 on the sundial refers to its completion date. The brick mansion is by the Thames next to St Mary's church and was in the family hands until Elizabeth Twining died on Christmas Day, 1889. Following her wish, it became a vicarage, the existing one being in such a dilapidated state that it was demolished, and the dial, with the motto 'Redeeming the time', dates from then. Since 2001 it has belonged to the Bishop of Kingston.

Five miles north of Dial House is Osterley Park, half way to Heathrow on the Piccadilly line. The National Trust describes Osterley as "*one of*  *the last surviving country estates in London*". Indeed it does look like an agricultural estate. There are rural vistas across many acres of arable fields that supply a well-stocked and inexpensive farm shop. Beside its tree-lined drive is a horse paddock and, most picturesquely, a large herd of Charolais cattle that has grown used to visitors. The house and estate were built by three generations of the Child family who were heavily involved in the East India Company as directors, stockholders and shipowners: three East Indiamen were named *Osterley*.

Sir Francis Child, one time Lord Mayor of London, was a goldsmith, and his connections with the Company gave him access to diamonds and other precious stones from India that led him to become 'jeweller in ordinary' to William III to whom he lent pieces for his coronation in 1689. He was also founder of the family business, Child & Co, which became the Company's banker. It remains one of London's oldest private banks, with a head office at 1 Fleet Street, though now owned by the Royal Bank of Scotland. In 1713 Francis Child, who lived in Hollybush House in Parsons Green, obtained Osterley on the default of a mortgage. The original Tudor house had been built for Sir Thomas Gresham, founder of the Royal Exchange, and although Sir Francis never lived there, he had it remodelled by William Chambers, who had designed the interior of Clive's house in Berkeley Square. Francis' son Robert continued the work on Osterley but it was Francis' grandson, Francis Child II, a director of the East India Company, who laid out the gardens and employed Robert Adam to create what would be his masterpiece, inspired like much of Claremont not by the East but in the prevailing fashion of the Classical world of Greece and Rome. Adam's work continued under Francis II's brother Robert, who was Chairman of the East India Company.

The interior has been renovated by the National Trust to look as it might have done in the 1780s, when the Childs used the house to impress their clients. To re-create this atmosphere a 'pop-up dining experience' was arranged in 2014 by The Art of Dining. The Long Room was decked about with silks and flowers, and as 'prospective patrons' of the East India Trading Company, it promised guests, "*Robert Child will attempt to curry your favour and secure your investment during a sumptuous five-course dinner.*"

This came at the end of 'The Trappings of Trade' exhibition put on at Osterley by the National Trust, with Chinese lacquered chests, Gujarati fabrics and

Chinese armorial porcelain, to show how luxury objects brought from Asia by the Company affected Georgian and Victorian tastes.

Dozens of mansions around Britain can look to the East India Company as their style-maker at some stage. If not the buildings themselves, then certainly some of their goods and chattels would have an Asiatic influence, for anybody who was well connected would have access to the Company and its fashionable imports, and could always find a way round any restrictions put on items such as silk. China particularly caught the public imagination, and the wealthy with friends in the right places gave them designs and drawings of what they wanted. These would be passed to the porcelain and furniture workshops of Jingdezhen and Canton at the start of the trading season and be ready for collection by the time the ships were homeward bound. From all parts of Asia where the Company traded it could source inexpensive custom-made boxes and cabinets, hand-painted wallpaper, finished silks and cottons for bedspreads and curtains, screens and fans, ivory and silver, camphor chests and furniture of rattan, ebony and rosewood. Designs for China might include local English scenes, family crests or copies of the fashionable Delftware. The domestic interiors from Elizabethan to Victorian times that have been re-created at the Geffrye Museum in Shoreditch show how much middle-class Londoners' taste was affected by these imports.

Eighteenth- and nineteenth-century hand-painted Chinese silk wallpaper can still be found in London, though not all of it is on public view. There is a pristine example in the Drawing Room of the Merchant Taylors' Guild in Threadneedle Street, around the corner from East India House and its auction rooms through which it my well have have arrived.

'The East India Company at Home, 1757–1857' was a project carried out by Warwick University and University College London between 2011 and 2014 to look at English country houses such as Osterley and how their tastes were influenced by  the Company. Woburn Abbey, home of the China-loving dukes of Bedford, was the venue for an exhibition they mounted in 2014 titled 'Peeling Back the Years: Chinoiserie at Woburn Abbey'. Henry Holland had designed a Chinese dairy, and the Chinese pagoda in the maze was based on the one at Kew by William Chambers. The Russell family, from whom the Bedfords sprang, established Howlands Wharf in Rotherhithe, owned East Indiamen and had a long association with the Company.

Valentines Mansion was another subject of the universities' project. If London were a clock face with its centre on Leadenhall Street, at ten past eight the hour hand would be on the Company men's mansions of south-west London and the minute hand would be on their mansions in Essex, at the edge of Epping Forest. Valentines is here, on the east side of the North Circular and five minutes' walk from Gants Hill in Zone 4 of the Central Line.

This Georgian mansion had its illustrious heyday when it was bought in 1754 by Charles Raymond who had joined the Company at sixteen and had his first command of an East Indiaman at twenty-one. As he prospered, so he moved out of town, from Wapping to West Ham and finally to Valentines, by which time he had become a successful ship owner. He was involved with Francis Child III in the first of three Indiamen to take the *Osterley* name, and the fortunes he made were used to turn Valentines into a stately home.

In 2007 it was fully restored under a Heritage Lottery Fund. For an exhibition in the dovecote two years later, Kathy Taylor, a local artist interested in colonial history, created an installation of 10,000 used teabags to represent the Company's trade, and re-created a British East India Company flag of 1707–1801, which some see as a precursor of the Stars and Stripes. Made of Indian cotton, it was appropriately dyed with tea and with indigo, which she bought from L Cornelissen & Son. Most intriguingly it used dye that had been extracted from red sanders wood or sandalwood, *Pterocarpus santalinus,* found among scraps of cargo of the *Valentine,* an East Indiaman owned by Raymond and built by Perry of Blackwall. She had run aground in a storm off the island of Sark on a return journey form India. The wreck had been identified in 1976 and some of the cargo, such as the red sandalwood, has been salvaged. Taylor's work was unambiguously titled *Stain.*

The North Circular today divides Valentines from its former neighbour, Wanstead House, coincidentally the seat of another Child family essential in the Company history, though unrelated to the Childs – should that be Children? – of Osterley. Wanstead House in what is now Wanstead Park in the London

Borough of Redbridge was the home of Sir Josiah Child, a wealthy merchant banker who in 1681 became one of the Company's most powerful Governors, described by Thomas Babington Macaulay as "*the despot of Leadenhall Street*". He made much of his fortune supplying the navy, and was a fierce advocate of the Company's monopoly trade. It was his granddaughter, Elizabeth Howland, who married into the Bedford family, bringing a dowry large enough to establish a shipbuilding business at Rotherhithe.

Sir Josiah's imperious, primping figure in Roman dress and full-bottom wig dominates his flamboyant funerary monument in St Mary's, once on the estate and now Wanstead parish church. The house was pulled down in 1823, and the Park was bought in 1880 as part of Epping Forest by the City of London, which is still responsible for its maintenance. Almost nothing remains as a reminder of Child's magnificent creation.

When Child purchased the property in 1763, it was called Wanstead Hall, and it had been a favourite retreat of Henry VII. Though Child bought the estate, he still could not buy acceptance among the aristocracy, and like Clive he was viewed as an uncultured upstart, no matter that he created an extravagant 300-acre garden planted with many tree-lined avenues with a chain of lakes and canals that caused it to be compared to  Versailles. Though he made a tidy profit investing in the Company, the diarist John Evelyn was not fooled by this show of wealth, describing Child as "*making fishponds many miles in circuit in Epping Forest in a barren spot as commonly these overgrown and suddenly monied men for the most part seat themselves. He from an ordinary merchant's apprentice & management of the East India Company's common stock being arrived to an estate of 'tis said £200,000 pounds... This merchant most sordidly avaricious, etc."*

The 'sordidly avaricious' aspersion cast on the Child name disappeared when his children married well. On inheriting the estate, his third son, Robert, used his vast inheritance to have the architect Colen Campbell entirely rebuild the manor into what was by all accounts one of the grandest Palladian houses around London. Created Viscount Castlemaine and, through marriage, First Earl Tylney, he took his place in high society, which he immortalised by commissioning William Hogarth to paint *The Assembly at Wanstead*. Now in the Philadelphia Museum of Art, the picture celebrates the twenty-fifth wedding anniversary of Lord and Lady Castlemaine who are seen entertaining in the Long Room with guests drinking and playing cards.

The family luck ran out in 1805 when the estate was inherited by Catherine Tylney-Long, who, aged sixteen, became the richest non-royal in Britain. Among her many suitors was William Wellesley-Pole, son of India's Governor-General Richard Wellesley and nephew of the Duke of Wellington. An absolute cad of the first water, William claimed on their wedding day in St James's Piccadilly to have forgotten the ring, and Catherine was obliged to send for a jeweller to select one, which she paid for, just as she had paid for everything else. In ten years Wellesley-Pole went through the entire family fortune and more, before fleeing abroad pursued by creditors who eventually took possession of the mansion. The auction book, a thick volume, is on

display in Wanstead Park's Temple building, and any items that Sir Francis had acquired during his governorship of the Company were dispersed in a six-day sale.

The house was then immediately pulled down, and nothing of it remains, though its shape can vaguely be made out on Wanstead Golf Course, which lies beside Wanstead Park, the club house occupying the former stables. A map at the entrance to the Park overlays the Child House and Gardens with the Golf Course and Park. Too late to preserve any foundations of the house, the site has been designated a Grade II listed landscape.

Freely accessible, the Park has the feel of a common, with woodland, canal, ornamental waters and fishing ponds. A suburban escape and dog-walkers' delight, it seems a long way from Versailles.

CLUBS

Two clubs in London were started for Company men: the Oriental Club, now opposite Bond Street station in Stratford Place, and the East India Club in St James's Square. Both came late in the life of the Company and were more associated with the era of the Raj. Neither now has particularly strong links with India.

The Oriental Club was started in 1824 by officers in the Company who were not eligible to join the service clubs around St James's. Instead, it attracted anybody who had 'travelled east' and it still has reciprocal arrangements with a number of clubs in Asia. Its first home was in Hanover Square, purpose-built by Benjamin Dean Wyatt, who had worked for the Company's Secrets department in Calcutta and on his return had been taken on as secretary to a former Company man, the Duke of Wellington, the club's honorary president.

In 1962 the club sold up to developers, counted itself lucky and decamped to Stratford House at the end of a curious cul-de-sac off Oxford Street. A flag with an Indian elephant is the only external sign of the house's function. Much altered since Robert Adam designed the core of the original building, it is one of the most pleasant clubs in London. Its main reception rooms have paintings of Wellington and that 'most superior person' the Indian Viceroy Lord Curzon. There is an agreeable terrace garden outside the Calcutta Light Horse Bar, and a painting of Warren Hastings is at the  foot of the stairs that lead to thirty-two bedrooms.

The Oriental lost some of its Company connections when the East India Club was founded in St James's Square in 1849. The new club immediately showed its ambitions by inviting Major General Sir Charles Napier, commander of the Indian Army in the Bombay Presidency, and the Marquess of Dalhousie, the incumbent Governor-General of India who had secured the Koh-i-Noor diamond, to be its first patrons. They were the men of the moment, though both were later seen as acting above and beyond their brief, and were blamed by some for causing the rebellion that led to the 1857 Indian Mutiny and the Company's disappearance. Napier was the subject of a cartoon in *Punch*, a magazine that spawned a number of imitators in expatriate India. Sent to quell a rebellion in Sindh, Napier had ended up conquering it, prompting a cartoon with a single word punning Latin caption, *Peccavi*, meaning 'I have sinned' (Sindh). Read by all the clubbable people in London, *Punch* had been started by the social reformer Henry Mayhew, author of the seminal *London Labour and London Poor* (1851), who had been sent off to join the Company by his lawyer father and sailed to Calcutta as a midshipman.

As a meeting place for Company officers on leave and for those who had retired, the East India Club offered Asia hands a place to swap stories, and there were many newsworthy events to talk about during its first few years. But in the 20th century it needed to refocus its membership, so it amalgamated with the Devonshire, the Sports, the Public Schools and Eccentric clubs. The Clive Room still has paintings from the Raj and there are sixty-six bedrooms, not all with facilities, plus a suite. Members have to be nominated and elected, and among those who have signed up are Lord Coe and Nigel Farage. The all-male bastion was breached in 2014 when the Lord Mayor of London, Fiona Woolf, became an Honorary Member.

Both clubs have a formal dress code. Paid-up members of the general public with limited means and in whatever clothes they choose may otherwise care to try the India Club in the Aldwych, which can be found over the road from the High Commissioner's 1930s India House. Time has passed by this classic London institution. The club bar is on the first floor with a view over the street, the basic restaurant on the floor above. With Formica tables and bare boards, there is no pretence that this is a venue for quality cuisine, but it can count the writer Will Self among its fans. There is no licence and no corkage charge on bottles brought in. Upstairs are the lodgings of the Strand Continental Hotel, a name that sounds far too grand for what it offers. Really it is the Indian *Sub*continental Hotel: eighty pounds for a double room, sixty for a single, nothing en-suite, and twenty-five quid if you don't mind sharing with five others.

MUSEUMS

One of the biggest questions over London's lost global giant is: whatever happened to all the treasures and curiosities brought back from Asia by Company men and exhibited in the famous East India House museum? The answer is that they were dispersed, bit by bit, over more than a century. Plans for a permanent home for this capricious cabinet of curiosities included the building of a wonderful riverside Moghul emporium in Belvedere Road, next to County Hall on the South Bank, where the India Office had a depository. There were also bids to house the collection in East London, a more appropriate part of town, perhaps, given the Company's interests in the area. In *The India Museum*, a lone book on the subject, published in 1982, the concluding comment of the author, Ray Desmond, was that he hoped the museum collection had finally found a home at Hyde Park Corner where St George's Hospital was closing. Shortly afterwards, however, the Lansdowne Hotel was built on this prime site.

Yet it did find a home for a while. For more than half a century much of the collection was displayed in the Victorian grandeur of the Imperial Institute in South Kensington. It had by then come under the care of the South Kensington Museum, and in 1899 was renamed the Victoria & Albert Museum. This visitor attraction had a mention in every guide book to London and it was taken as a permanent fixture in the city's cultural life. But the building was pulled down in 1956 and no place could be found for a collection that by this time seemed redolent of the mischief of the Company and an out-of-date empire that had just let go of India, the jewel in its crown.

The museum in Leadenhall Street had been started at the beginning of the nineteenth century as an extension of the Company's library. It soon amassed a motley number of items, from natural history and hand-made objects to important archaeological finds, all shipped back by Company men. There were elephant heads, Chinese miniatures, weapons and devotional objects, and most famously there was

Tipu's Tiger, made for the Sultan of Mysore and the most extraordinary item of booty from the siege of Seringapatam (see next chapter), now permanently on display in the V&A. This life-size mechanical toy shows a tiger mauling an East India Company soldier who puts his hand to his mouth in horror and groans when a handle is turned, pumping air into a pipe organ. There were stories of people fainting on encountering the grisly entertainment.

The public's appetite for curiosities from the farthest corners of the expanding world had been whetted with the Great Exhibition in Hyde Park, at which the East India Company was by far the largest exhibitor. Soon afterwards the Leadenhall Street collection was attracting 100,000 visitors a year.

On the Company's demise and the imminent demolition of East India House, responsibility for the collection was borne by the government's new India

Office in Whitehall. Discussions naturally took place with the British Museum, but first off the blocks was Joseph Hooker, who rushed up from Kew and carted away what he could from the basement, taking what he thought salvageable from among the rotting piles of specimens and flaking pressed plants, not to mention thirty-six tons of wood samples and three tons of rice trials. This was not only for Kew's herbarium and library, but also for the Museum of Economic Botany, which Joseph's father, William, had started in the Georgian building known as 'Museum No.1', which is still open beside the pond opposite the main Palm House. The 'Plants and Peoples' exhibition on the ground floor continues to show natural materials from the East and how they are

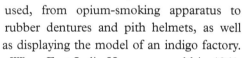

used, from opium-smoking apparatus to rubber dentures and pith helmets, as well as displaying the model of an indigo factory.

When East India House was sold in 1861, items of immediate value such as jewellery, coins, medals and miniatures, went for auction, while the vast quantity of books, illustrations and written archives was destined for the British Museum Library. The remaining bulk of material left the City for Whitehall, where it found a temporary home at Fife House in Whitehall Yard, while the India Office was being completed across the road. Items were crammed into the rooms of what had been the riverside residence of Britain's longest-serving Prime Minister, Lord Liverpool. Statues of the Company's generals and governors greeted visitors in the hall, and the garden was used for sculptures and archaeological finds. The most important of these were second-century AD marbles and sculptures from the Great Stupa at Amaravati, which had been excavated by Colin Mackenzie, the Company's first Surveyor General of India. The initial consignment reached London in 1816, and later finds arrived just a few months before East India House was demolished.

In the meantime the trend for world fairs started by the Great Exhibition led to further expositions in South Kensington and in Paris. With a continuing interest in promoting trade, the India Office ensured a large presence of manufactured and agricultural products, for which around half of the cost was expected to come from India. When Wyatt's India Office building finally opened, it was supposed to be a depository for the collection, but accommodation was desperately cramped, and in 1879 it was prepared for a final dispersal. The British Museum had already taken some of the zoological collection, and now it took what was left to form the basis of its planned Natural History Museum in South Kensington. The Indian Institute, which had just been inaugurated as part of Oxford University to train civil servants for work in the Raj, took material. Other items went to the India Museum in Calcutta. But craft and cultural artefacts, principally the textiles and decorative arts that made up the largest part of the collection, were handed over by the India Office to the custody of the Science and Arts Department of the Committee of the Council of Education in South Kensington where an Indian collection was already established.

It took two curators two years to catalogue the 19,066 items. The resulting *Inventory of the Collection of Examples of Indian Art and Manufacturing*

Transferred to the South Kensington Museum is in two volumes. It includes silk and cotton scarves, turbans, handkerchiefs, caps, shawls and pyjamas, prayer wheels and twelve pages of idols, details of bettel-nut cutters, arms and armour, bows and battle-axes, models of carriages, conveyances and bullock carts, lathes, looms, saddles, carpets, rugs, jewellery,  anklets, armlets, toe rings, gongs, tambourines and fiddles, hookahs, puzzles, snuff boxes, miniatures and mannequins, maps and plans, fishing nets and farm implements.

The best of these were selected to fill the ten rooms earmarked as the India Museum in the east wing of the new Imperial Institute opposite, in Exhibition Road. T.E. Collcutt, architect of the Savoy Hotel and the Palace Theatre, had been chosen to provide a neo-Renaissance building in keeping with the surrounding museum buildings. The Eastern Galleries were at the centre of the 600-foot frontage, and the Amaravati sculptures provided a dramatic entrance. These archaeological treasures had escaped the British Museum's haul of thirty-seven cases of Assyrian and Indian sculpture from East India House, from where they had also acquired a tessellated Roman pavement that the Company had discovered beneath the Leadenhall Street building when it was extended.

In the Imperial Institute's entrance hall were shopfronts and house façades to be seen in India. A large collection of clay figures, showing races, castes and occupations of Asian people had been originally shown at the Great Exhibition. There were many models of cities and temples, and highlights included seven cases of treasure from the King of Burma's palace at Mandalay and the golden throne of Maharajah Runjeet Singh, now on display in the V&A, which Lord Dalhousie had sent home after the Company's nine-day auction of the treasury in

Lahore. There were also oil paintings on canvas of the extraordinary cave murals from Ajanta, dating from the second century BC and the oldest in India. The originals of these were painted by Major Robert Gill who had joined the India Army at the age of nineteen, and spent thirty years investigating the caves. The V&A still has eighty-one canvases and these have been the subject of a recent conservation programme.

The India Museum was a central part of 'Albertopolis', the group of educational buildings dreamed of by Prince Albert for South Kensington, and it remained here for two generations until it got

in the way of Imperial College's expansion plans. All that now remains is the Queen's Tower and two lions at its feet; its bells are still rung, but the viewing platform is no longer open. The role of the Imperial Institute was transferred to the Commonwealth Institute in Holland Park, and since its closure its remaining functions have been directed from offices in New Zealand House.

The V&A is universally recognised as having an unsurpassed textile collection, which is dipped into for regular major exhibitions and tours with Indian themes. In collaboration with the National Museum of

India, it has digitised 2,000 'Company' paintings from India that catered to Western taste, giving snapshots of local life. Its permanent gallery of souvenirs from the Company are informative, explaining how they came to be custom made for their British buyers. Some are donations from private collections, from families whose forebears headed east, and many give tantalising glimpses of tastes and lifestyles. Among the ivory and hardwood furniture, for instance, is a sideboard with a depiction of Montagu House, the first home of the British Museum, and English scenes incongruously decorate China ware. There is ingenious craftsmanship, too. A large ivory sailing ship has clockwork oarsmen, and Tipu's Tiger is still popular, though its mechanism has not been tried for some time.

Meanwhile the Amaravati sculptures have come to rest in the British Museum's Asia rooms where they occupy a special corner behind glass doors. The museum also has a large collection of coins minted by the Company in India and now valuable collectors' items. In 2013 the first Indian silver rupee from the Company's Bombay Mint, dated 1839, sold at auctioneers Baldwins in the Strand for £132,000, an unprecedented six-figure sum. Coins were among the collection of Claudius James Rich, who in 1808 at the age of twenty-one had been appointed the Company's Resident in Baghdad. The large number of antiquities that were bought directly from him by the British Museum in 1825 became the foundation of its Mesopotamian collection.

Many items held by the museum's Department of Asia would have arrived on East Indiamen, but one item it did not have for its 2013 exhibition 'Shunga: Sex and Pleasure in Japanese Art, 1600–1900' was the earliest examples of *shunga* known in the West. These

erotic illustrations were brought by John Saris, Chief Factor of the Company's factory, or trading post, in Java and captain of the East Indiaman *Clove*, the first Western ship to visit Japan. He reached his destination in 1613 bearing gifts of wool and a telescope for the shogun, Tokugawa Hidetada, who allowed him to establish a trading post at Hirado, on Japan's southernmost island. The shogun's gifts for James I included two Japanese suits of armour. One is now in 'Fit for a King', the Royal Armouries' permanent collection in the Tower of London, and the other is on loan to the Royal Armouries' Oriental Collection in Leeds.

Saris also brought back lacquers and screens to be sold at the Company's first auction, which was also said to be the world's first auction of art objects. In December 2014, for the 400th anniversary of the return of the *Clove*, Bonhams New Bond Street held a special Japanese art auction. But Saris' *shunga* erotic prints never went to auction. The Directors had been less than pleased to see them, describing them as '*a great scandall*' and they had them publicly burned. Saris never worked for the Company again.

Another anniversary celebration in 2014 was a musical evening in All Saints church in Fullham, where Saris is buried in the chancel. Japanese and English music from his times was played and the BBC's Evan Davis read from *Clove*'s log.

The Hirado factory lasted no more than a decade,

and not long afterwards Japan closed its doors on trade with the West for more than two centuries. So hazy was the seventeenth-century idea of the world, that when the shogun armour was put on display in the Tower of London in 1662 it was described as 'the armour of the Great Moghul', a title the treasure apparently retained for centuries.

The Tower was just one home for items from the armoury in Leadenhall Street. Initially, the collection was transported to the new United Services Museum in Whitehall Yard, from where it was dispersed. A natural home might have been the National Maritime Museum, but this was not set up in Greenwich until nearly a century after the Company had folded. The museum was based on the 19th-century Royal Navy collection, and until the Navy left Greenwich in 1998, it devoted much of its space to the age of Nelson and the explorations of James Cook. In 2005, however, the  museum received a donation large enough to allow it to undergo major reconstruction. The benefactor was Romanian-born Sammy Ofer, who had served in the Royal Navy during the war, and subsequently founded a shipping company in Israel, now one of the largest in the world. In reconfiguring the galleries in the new wing, the first floor was used for a permanent exhibition: 'Traders: the East India Company and Asia', which focused on the Indian Ocean. This was balanced ge fographically by another permanent exhibition on the same floor: 'The Atlantic: Slavery, Trade, Empire', to which a third will be added with the new Pacific galleries, due to open in 2018.

Sammy Ofer died in June 2011, just three months

before the Traders exhibition opened. Dipping into its own collections and using long-term loans, the museum has been able to provide a narrative of John Company that addresses

its sins as well as its glamour, starting with a fine three-quarter portrait of Sir James Lancaster, leader of the Company's first voyage, which is identical to the one that hangs in the Skinners' Company in the City. But perhaps the most telling painting in the museum's collection is of the three Money brothers, who made their fortunes in the East. In the foreground is a map; in the background is the East Indiaman *Rose* for which the oldest brother, William Taylor, in the blue uniform of a lieutenant, has just received his first commission. His arm leans on the youngest, Robert, who points to Canton, while middle brother, James, indicates Calcutta. The painting is by John Francis Rigaud and was commissioned by the Blackwall ship owner and Company Director Sir Robert Wigram, a friend of their father, William, who was also Director, as his son, William, would later become. It conveys both the romance of the Company and the cosy fraternity that held it together.

Dr Robert Blyth, the exhibition's curator and co-author of the accompanying book, *Monsoon Traders*, says that although the history of the Company has generated a lot of media interest in recent years, he is not certain what impact the Traders gallery has had on public awareness of the EIC.

"Visitors seem to enjoy the gallery, and feedback has been mainly positive," he says. "It is clear from our comment cards that they do engage with some of the issues raised by the display."

THE EIC ARMY

"*I have not a clue who they are or what they did,*" Ken Livingstone, the Mayor of London, told the Greater London Assembly in 2000. He was talking about the two bronze statues that occupy the large plinths in the southern corners of Trafalgar Square. He knew that on the north side a third statue, of a man dressed as a Roman emperor on a horse, was George IV, while the empty fourth plinth had just been used for what would become an annual art installation. He now wondered if these two unknowns shouldn't step down to make way for more popular figures.

"*I imagine that not one person in 10,000 going through Trafalgar Square knows any details about the lives of those two generals,*" he said.

Both were, in fact, heroes from the India Army at the time of the Mutiny, known in India as the First War of Independence. Moustachioed and mutton-chopped, Sir Henry Havelock stands on a plinth that bears a dedication to the General and "*...his brave companions in arms during the campaign in India 1857*". But nothing links the other General, Sir Charles James Napier, with India. The bronze of

Napier, that early patron of the East India Club, stands six-foot tall, with curling locks and steadfast gaze, in the south-west corner. He and the poet

Tennyson were described by their Regent Street optician as being the two most short-sighted men in Britain. This defect did not seem to hamper his career, nor did the fact that he was a cousin of the Whig Charles James Fox, who campaigned against the corruption of the East India Company. Napier had served in the Napoleonic Wars in Spain and Portugal before, aged sixty, he was made Major General of the Bombay Presidency, in 1842. The scroll he holds in his right hand is the symbol of his governorship of Sindh, today part of Pakistan, where his action had supplied the *Punch* cartoonist with the pun for his sins. He commanded a loyal following among his troops, and soldiers paid the bulk of the public subscription for the statue.

Napier died at his home, Oaklands, now a school, in Portsmouth, in 1853, and was buried there in Domus Dei, the Royal Garrison Church. He was still suffering from wounds he had received at the Battle of Corunna during the Peninsular War. British troops in Spain were under the command of Sir John Moore, who was killed at Corunna in the hour of victory, and the poem by Charles Grey of his expeditious burial (*"Not a drum was heard, not a funeral note, As his corse to the rampart we hurried..."*) is a high spot in the literature of British military history.

At the start of the Napoleonic Wars, Sir John had been in charge of the defences of south-east England, training light infantry troops, building Martello towers and digging the defensive Royal Military Canal across Romney Marsh. Napier was stationed here too, and had a barracks named after him. And so was William Havelock, the older brother of Henry. A month after he had done his duty in the Light Division at the Battle of Waterloo, William helped Henry, who had been studying law, to enter the army. In 1823, aged twenty-seven, Henry embarked on the East Indiaman *Captain Kid* for India, where through his Baptist wife he discovered an enthusiasm for religion, distributing Bibles to his troops. After serving in campaigns in Afghanistan and Burma, General Henry Havelock found lasting fame during the Indian Rebellion of 1857, when he cut a swathe through the mutineers in Uttar Pradesh, recaptured Cawnpore and lifted the siege at Lucknow where he died of dysentery.

Havelock and Napier stand in the shadow of that great admiral Horatio Nelson on a square completed in 1844 to commemorate his victory over the French and Spanish off Cape Trafalgar thirty-nine years earlier. Some East Indiamen had been commandeered during the Napoleonic Wars; others fought it out by themselves, notably in the Battle of Pulo Aura, which turned out to be more of an encounter than a fight. At the beginning of 1804, the year before Trafalgar, the annual China Fleet of merchantmen was heading home from Canton. Included in the convoy of sixteen lightly armed East Indiamen were eleven 'country ships' trading between China and India. On board the *Earl of Camden* was the fleet's Commodore, Nathaniel Dance, grandson of the City of London architect George Dance the Elder and one of the Company's most experienced commanders. Knowing that they might encounter the French fleet, before embarking Dance ordered Royal Navy blue ensigns to be carried and had the ships painted to look like frigates, with enlarged gun ports. A French squadron under Rear-Admiral Count Linois caught up with the fleet at dusk on February 15 in the Strait of Malacca. Outnumbered and outgunned, Dance ordered the blue ensigns to be hoisted and brought the fleet into lines of battle. Taken in by this deception, and convinced that he had met a far superior Royal Navy force, Linois took off after a brief exchange of fire, and was pursued so tenaciously through the night that he eventually created a smoke screen to lose his foe. Having saved a lot of people a great deal of money, Dance and his captains and their crews were rewarded a total of £50,000 by the Directors of the Company. Dance also received a pension of £500 a year, a knighthood and £3,000 from the Bombay Insurance Company.

The *Warren Hastings*, one of the largest Company ships, was not so lucky. Sailing to China in June 1806 she became separated from the two ships accompanying her, and she was intercepted and captured by a French frigate, who took her as a prize to Mauritius, though she was later recaptured by the Royal Navy.

The sea war with France was largely over after Trafalgar, when a new hero arrived on the battlefields of Europe. As Trafalgar Square is to Nelson, so Hyde Park Corner is to Arthur Wellesley, 1st Duke of Wellington. Apsley House, his London home, stood by the toll gate where the main road left Westminster for the west, and its address was simply No.1 London. Today the building is filled with the astonishing trophies of Wellington's wars with

Napoleon, including an outsized nude figure of the French Emperor as Mars the Peacemaker by Canova. The Duke might have good reason to be grateful to him, for without the Napoleonic Wars, his titles and decorations would have been far fewer, his life far poorer, and he might have been just another half-forgotten Indian army officer in Trafalgar Square, perhaps occupying the fourth plinth.

There is barely a mention of Wellington's India campaigns in Apsley House. There is a single full-length portrait of his older brother Richard, 1st Marquess Wellesley, who was Governor General of India and had been famous long before Arthur. It was Richard who had bought Apsley House after his return to London. Their father was an Irish peer, Lord  Mornington, a musician and spendthrift who lost the family estates. Richard eventually inherited the title that comes from a village in County Meath, and the name was given to Mornington Crescent in north London, after their sister, Anne, married the local landowner and developer Henry Fitzroy.

Richard Wellesley was a classics scholar and a confidant of William Pitt the Younger. Though apparently vain and highly ambitious, his political career was blighted by poor health, financial worries and an inappropriate relationship with a French actress. Although in later life he would be entirely overshadowed by Arthur, the two brothers were always close, and when finances were thin, Richard put Apsley House up for sale. Arthur, flush with success at Waterloo, put in a sealed bid, not wanting to cause embarrassment with a direct financial proposal. The Duke then had the house enlarged by the architect Benjamin Dean Wyatt, who had been employed in the Company's Political and Secrets Department in Calcutta during Richard's time there. The extensions included the State Dining Room and the Waterloo Gallery where banquets were held each year on the anniversary of the battle. Apsley House is still in the family's hands. The Wellingtons, whose dukes live in Stratfield Saye House in Hampshire, a palatial estate given to the first duke by a grateful nation, occupy the basement, and the Wellesleys the top floor, while the Morningtons are happily housed elsewhere. On the coronation of Elizabeth II in 1952, the family gathered on the portico to watch the royal procession and, nearly 150 years after they had been brought back from India, to drink the last two bottles of Madeira that Richard had taken to India on his appointment as Governor-General.

The Napoleonic Wars were not confined to Europe, and the recent loss of the American colonies had freed officers and troops to serve in other parts of the world where Anglo-French hostilities threatened to break out. Arthur Wellesley, raised to the rank of colonel, arrived in Calcutta with the 33rd Regiment in 1796, and Lord Richard Wellesley's appointment as Governor-General the following year ensured his rapid promotion. The Fourth Anglo-Mysore War was underway and Richard ordered the army to attack the Mysore capital on the fortified river island of Seringapatam. Here was the palace of Tipu, the Tiger of Mysore, the last Mughal emperor of Southern India, a Suni who governed a Hindu majority in the subcontinent's most prosperous state, with trading established around the Persian

Gulf. After three wars to maintain control of the region, the first under his father, Hyder Ali, Tipu had developed an unalloyed hatred of the British whom he had defeated at the Battle of Pollilur in 1780, one of the Company's severest setbacks, when 7,000 were taken prisoner and 3,000 killed, many by Mysorean rockets that showed Tipu's army to be technologically more advanced than the British. Sword blades were attached to the rockets that could be fired over a kilometre, savagely scything through the air. Examples can be seen in 'Firepower', the Royal Artillery Museum in Woolwich, where the Royal Arsenal later developed the technology.

A scholarly and highly capable leader, Tipu had adopted the tiger as his emblem, and had big cats carved and painted all around his palace and city. Howitzers were shaped like crouching tigers and tiger  heads were cast on the mouths of his cannon. His furnishings and clothes were tiger-striped, and live tigers guarded the palace doors. Such a colourful, charismatic figure made him an easily demonised enemy, especially when it was known he was seeking an alliance with France.

Colonel Wellesley's regiment was deployed as part of a division in the British East India Company army commanded by Major-General George Harris. There were around 4,000 European troops in the Company army, and 26,000 native sepoys (privates). Another 25,000 troops were supplied by the Nizam of neighbouring Hyderabad, including 16,000 cavalry. Tipu Sultan's forces are estimated to have been around just over half the British total. The assault was led by Major-General David Baird, a veteran of the Mysore wars, who had spent four years as a prisoner of Tipu's father. On May 2 1799, batteries fired by the Nizam of Hyderabad's troops opened a breach in the city wall. Two days later, at 11am, troops stormed the citadel, and by dusk the place was taken. Tipu Sultan lay where he had fought to the death. Some 9,000 of his troops were dead, and there were just 350 British casualties.

Over the next few days of indiscriminate rape, pillage and plunder, the whole city was turned over. Colonel Arthur Wellesley, placed by his brother in charge of the city and established in Tipu's palace, wrote to their mother: '*Scarcely a house in the town was left unplundered... I came in to take command of the army on the 5th and with greatest exertion, by hanging, flogging etc etc in the course of that day restored order.*'

Lady Mornington must have been proud of him. More than a million pounds of prize money was distributed among the victors. Colonel Wellesley ordered all Tipu's personal belongings to be returned to England to prevent them being used as "*sacred relics of Tipu Sultan the Martyr, to mobilise the people against the British*". Tipu's beautiful chintz tent was taken by Robert Clive's son, Edward, a Company Administrator, and it can now be seen at Powis Castle. Wellesley took for himself a sword and dagger belonging to Tipu, and they are displayed in a small case at Apsley House, the only visible evidence here of his whole time in India. Visitors to No.1 London may be forgiven for not knowing that he had ever been in India at all.

A Prize Agent was appointed to break up the booty, described by contemporary sources as '*seldom, if ever surpassed, as to amount, by any conquest of the British army*'. Tipu's library and collection of manuscripts was of particular value. Some of the greatest treasures from Seringapatam were disposed between the Company's Directors and the Royal Family, and Hyder Ali's favourite sword is still in the Royal Collection. But a British monarch never had the opportunity of sitting on Tipu's fabulous throne. Following Colonel Wellesley's concerns, and to the regret of the Directors, who wanted to present it to George III, it was broken up with sledgehammers.

Seringapatam's extraordinary treasures are scattered among the world's museums, and more than two centuries after the siege they are still sale-room regulars, often appearing in Bonhams' twice-yearly auctions of Islamic and Indian Art in London. Two gem-set golden tiger finials from the throne came on sale in 2009 and 2010, fetching £389,600 and £434,400. But the biggest modern sale of Seringapatam booty fetched more than £6 million. This was largely the collection of Robin Wigington, who came from a family of Birmingham gun manufacturers and spent a lifetime studying and amassing Tipu's armaments for the Armouries Museum he set up in Stratford-upon-Avon. He died in 2003, and in 2015, after the museum had decided to redirect its focus, the collection was sold at Bonhams. A jewel-encrusted sword with a tiger's head pommel from Tipu's royal regalia went for £2,154,500, and a three-pounder cannon with field carriage made £1,426,500, including the seller's commission. There was also

a gem-set jade plaque in a box with a fading, hand-written note: *'Taken from the body of Tipoo Sultan after he was killed 1799'*. It has been said that if Tipu had been encumbered with the amount of jewellery and weaponry supposed to have been taken from his warm corpse, it was a miracle he had been able to stand up under the weight of it all.

Apart from the mechanical tiger, the V&A also has the Seringapatam Jewels, which are on loan from the Harris (Belmont) Charity. Lucy, wife of the cricketing fourth Lord Harris, who was made Governor of Bombay in 1890, enjoyed wearing the emeralds on their tours. The Harris charity runs Belmont House near Faversham in Kent, which Major-General Harris purchased in 1801 with prize money from Seringapatam. There are tours of the house, designed by Samuel Wyatt, and the fourteen-acre gardens of the family estate are open to the public in summer. Prospect Tower, a folly built for Harris in the garden, sleeps two and can be rented.

Another treasure that Major-General Harris acquired at Seringapatam was a pendant with a 38-carat emerald surrounded by topaz, sapphire, ruby, diamond and pearl. It did not remain in the family's hands, and in 2011, still in its original setting, it was sold at Bonhams with the contents of the St Lucia home of Colin Tennant, Lord Glenconner, for £217,250.

Baird, a Scot who would go on to become second-in-command to Sir John Moore at Corunna, was aggrieved that Lord Richard Wellesley had passed him over in favour of brother Arthur, but the Directors did not let the Wellesleys have it all their own way. They rejected the proposal of the appointment of Henry, the youngest of the Wellesley brothers, as resident of Lucknow, and they refused a Company staff salary that Lord Wellesley requested for Arthur at Mysore in addition to his army pay.

Promoted to Major-General, Arthur went on to further victory against a much larger force at the Battle of Assaye in the Second Anglo-Maratha War, so that by the time the brothers left India, in March 1805, the Company's empire was a bigger place. They arrived back in London in September, a month before the Battle of Trafalgar. Shortly afterwards, Arthur Wellesley had an appointment with the Secretary of State at the Colonial Office. He was kept waiting for forty-five minutes, as was the other man in the room, Admiral Lord Nelson. It was the only time the two men met, and in his description of the encounter Wellington said that Nelson appeared "*vain and silly*" until he was informed who he was addressing, when he became sensible and "*talked like an officer and a gentleman*". If not yet as famous as Nelson, Wellesley already had a reputation forged in India.

In the City, the Company's patriotic support for the nation's wars against France and its concerns about the effects of the French Revolution produced the Royal East India Volunteers, made up of the Company's warehousemen and other manual workers who would parade about the streets. The first two regiments were organised in 1797 "*to more effectually secure the Warehouses of the Company against hazard from Insurrection or Tumults*". There would be gun and bayonet practices and shows of military skills in various parts of London, while their bands would play specially composed marches. In July 1797 the Second Regiment was reviewed in Lord's Cricket Ground at its original Dorest Fields site, in front of Company

Directors, Lord Richard Wellesley and Prime Minister William Pitt. Maintained at a cost of around £20,000 a year, the volunteers were joined by a third regiment to make a complement of some 1,500, and were disbanded once Napoleon had been defeated.

The relationship between the Company's Army and the Royal Army was always close, as their aims were generally mutual, especially during European conflicts, such as the Seven Years' War with France (1756–63) when Clive was in India, and the Napoleonic Wars (1799–1815) in the Wellesley era. When the Company disbanded, the EIC army was seamlessly absorbed into Britain's Indian Army, and both the National Army Museum in Chelsea and the Royal Artillery Museum in Woolwich have East India Company material in their collections. The Indian Army's contribution in the two world wars was crucial, providing 1.5 million recruits in 1914 and, by 1945, 2.5 million, the largest volunteer force in history. Independence in 1947 meant that Britain lost a large part of its military might.

From the beginning, the Company had a need for armed protection for its forts and factories, and to give it muscle when negotiating trade agreements. In the early days sailors had to be prepared to engage in land skirmishes, but the Company also developed a separate armed navy in India, which by the 1680s had become known as the Bombay Marine. Intended to rid the sea of 'pirates', it operated mainly around the west coast of India in the Arabian Sea, backing up land-based military action by the Company. In spite of its successes, it was never highly regarded, and when in 1755 Commander William James cleared the seas for trade by destroying the Maharatha Tulagee Angria's island fort of Suvarnadurg on the Malibar coast eighty miles south of Bombay, he was awarded a meagre £100. James' knowledge of the local waters, however, made him invaluable in London. A Welsh miller's son, he went on to become Chairman of the Company, a member of the Royal Society and a baronet. His portrait by Sir Joshua Reynolds hangs in the National Maritime Museum in Greenwich. He purchased a country estate nearby in Eltham, and after his sudden death during his daughter's wedding celebrations, his wife employed the Company's architect, Richard Jupp, to build a folly as a memorial. Suvarnadurg was anglicised to Severndroog, and Severndroog Castle on the top of Shooter's Hill is today open to the public.

On a clear day from its sixty-three-foot tower there is a view over London and, it is claimed, seven counties, but even with the binoculars provided it is a rare day when Windsor Castle can be identified.

Each of the three Presidencies built up its own army independently. Officers were invariably British, with native sepoy conscripts. The Company's ability to call on the Royal Army was first recorded in 1687 under James II, when a hundred soldiers of the Eleventh Foot embarked on the *Caesar* for Fort St George, Madras. A quarter of a century later the Company established Fort William in Calcutta with a standing garrison of 125, and after being overrun by French troops in 1746, it was considerably strengthened.

EIC foot and horse artillery regiments were added in 1748, the cavalry officers distinguished by their gold-braided blue jackets and Roman-style helmets with horse-hair plumes, dyed red. In the second half of the eighteenth century there was a dramatic increase in

the size of the Company forces and by 1806 the three standing armies amounted to 154,000. Ten years later, with rocket science improving, Captain William Whish established a camel-mounted division, the Bengal Rocket Troop, and a maquette of a trooper can be seen at 'Firepower', the Royal Artillery Museum in Woolwich. The museum's East India Company material is displayed in the first-floor History Gallery where there are two elegant bronze guns, one from Seringapatam, with a tiger's head, the other from the royal armoury in Lahore, with a carriage of brass, copper, steel and mother-of-pearl. The highly decorated great Bhurtpore Gun, captured during the Siege of Bhurtpore in 1826 and presented by the Company to George IV, stood outside the Woolwich barracks until the regiment left in 2007, taking it with them. It now stands on a plinth outside the Officers' Mess at the Royal School of Artillery in Larkhill on Salisbury Plain.

The Royal Military Academy at Woolwich trained the Company cadets until 1809 when increased demand led the Company to open its own military seminary at Addiscombe, one of Croydon's six ancient boroughs, birthplace of model Kate Moss and three tram stops from the mainline station at East Croydon.

Addiscombe Place was a manor house built in 1702 to a design by John Vanbrugh, with allegorical figures decorating the walls and ceiling of the grand staircase and first-floor salon by James Thornhill, artist of the Painted Hall in the Old Royal Naval College, Greenwich. It was purchased by the Company in 1808 along with eighty-eight acres of grounds for parades and training. Cadets were recruited from ages fourteen to sixteen, and they would remain for two years, studying to be engineers, surveyors, artillery officers and, later, infantry soldiers. Their curriculum covered

mathematics, natural philosophy and chemistry, 'the Hindustani, Latin and French languages' as well as civil, military and lithographic drawing and surveying. Surveying was always an important part of the Company's intelligence in India, and after Tipu's defeat the first major land survey was carried out, covering 40,000 miles and lasting nine years. The subsequent Great Trigonomical Survey, conducted throughout the subcontinent, identified the highest mountain in the world, which was named after Surveyor General George Everest, who had entered Addiscombe Military Seminary at the age of sixteen.

Detailed illustrations were essential to reconnaissance, and Addiscombe's teaching staff included Christian Schetky, Painter in Water Colours to the Duke of Clarence and Marine Painter to George IV. To mimic local conditions, pumps in a pond called the Coldstream caused turbulent waters across which cadets had to erect bridges and pontoons, while buildings were trialled in the Sand Modelling Hall. Engineers and surveyors at first used a *camera lucida* to help capture images, and in the seminary's last few years photography was also studied for use in the field. A number of these immaculate, detailed drawings and early photographs are now in the British Library.

Records of the Engineers of the Honourable East India Company Army from 1740 to 1862 are kept at the Royal Engineers Museum and Library in Gillingham, behind Chatham Dockyards in Kent. A priceless item in its collection is a set of 18th-century Sikh chain armour with gauntlet, helmet, breast and back plates dating from the mid-1700s. It came from the armoury of Maharajah Duleep Singh, and after his defeat it was brought to back from India by Lord Dalhousie to add to his collection. In 1898,

some thirty years after Dalhousie died, it was auctioned, and it was donated to the museum in 1959. There it languished until 2007 when a new curator, Lauren Jones, came across it in a store cupboard. It is too fragile to be exhibited but one night in September 2010 it was put on show in an unsuccessful campaign to raise money for its conservation.

Chatham was also the site of Brompton Barracks, the East India Company's army recruiting Depot before 1842 when it moved to a larger site at Warley, near Brentwood in Essex. This accommodated around a thousand soldiers who underwent training before setting off for India. The Ford Motor Company now has its UK headquarters on the Warley site by Clive Road. Opposite is the Company's Italianate chapel designed by Matthew Digby Wyatt, the Company's Surveyor and architect of India House in Whitehall. Grade II listed, it became the Chapel of the Essex Regiment, now absorbed in the Royal Anglian Regiment.

On the demise of the Company, Addiscombe Military Seminary was closed and sold to the fledgling British Land Company, now one of the largest developers in Britain with such prestigious buildings as 122 Leadenhall Street (Richard Rogers' 'Cheese Grater') in its £18 billion portfolio. Housing plots were allocated around five roads they named after Company men, though neither Canning, Elgin, Havelock or Outram had been pupils of the Seminary. The Seminary had room for around 150 boys, and at the time of its closure, thirty-four of the 151 resident cadets had been born in the 'East Indies'. Indeed, none of the cadets who ever attended the Seminary had lived within ten miles of it, nor had any of the first middle-class residents of these houses. All had servants, none were manual workers, no ale houses were allowed to be built and any kind of manufacturing was banned. There is a pub now, the Cricketer, up on Addiscombe Road, but there is no sign of the Company. Locals vaguely know about it, because of the street names, but it was too long ago. Only two buildings from the Seminary have survived in what is now Croydon's East India Estate Conservation Area. The 1851 Gymnasium in Havelock Road is Grade II listed and converted into flats, renamed Havelock Hall after the Major-General. Ashleigh 1 and 2 are in Clyde Road, named after Lord Clyde ("*As Commander-in-Chief in India he brought the Indian Mutiny to an end in 1858*" is inscribed on his statue in Waterloo Place off Pall Mall). These semi-detached houses were built for the Company's professors and are now labelled with a green Croydon Heritage plaque.

WRITERS

Sometimes it must have seemed as if East India House was awash with Indian ink as Writers scratched away at reports and directives, at orders and accounts, sales reports, letters and logs, no matter that it would be at least a year before any correspondence to Asia might receive a reply, even when using smaller, faster packet ships. To add to the toil and ensure safe delivery, the Company learned to send important dispatches in triplicate to be sent on three separate vessels in the hope that at least one would get through.

Writers were junior clerks, who could rise to become secretaries, superintendents, elders and examiners working in Leadenhall Street or taking up any number of administrative tasks in Asia. A London clerk could be identified by the stains on his fingers and the hardened lump on his middle finger where his quill pressed all day. He might also be recognised by his accent. The monopoly rights of the East India Company were written into the 1707 Act of Union, making them binding in all parts of the United Kingdom, and by the late 18th century a large percentage of the Writers in Leadenhall Street as well as in Asia were from Scotland. Robert Burns had an early unrealised desire to visit the Indies, East or West, and two of the poet's sons became Company men through the influence of a relative, James Shaw. Born in Kilmarnock, Shaw was a member of the Court of Proprietors and was elected Lord Mayor of London in 1805.

One English Writer who famously toiled away for nine hours a day, six days a week, for twenty-five years, from the age of seventeen until the day he retired in 1817, was the essayist and author Charles Lamb. His bronze bust can be seen on the side of St Sepulchre's in Giltspur Street, with the inscription *"Perhaps the most beloved name in literature"*. He  is wearing the bow tie and large-lapelled coat of a Bluecoat Boy, as for seven years he attended Christ's Hospital in nearby Newgate Street where Samuel Taylor Coleridge was a fellow pupil. The statue was moved here when the school relocated to the country.

Not much read today, Lamb was the popular author of biographical sketches titled *Essays of Elia*, a name he borrowed from another clerk in the Accountants Office where he worked, and *Tales from Shakespeare*, written for children.

A description of the clerks' office at East India House is given by Thomas de Quincy, author of *Confessions of an Opium Eater*, who one winter day in 1804 visited his friend Lamb unannounced. Having become lost among the labyrinthine, candle-lit corridors, he eventually found himself in a large room *"with a very lofty writing desk separated by a still higher railing from that part of the floor on which the profane – the laity like myself – were allowed to approach the clerus, a clerkly ruler of the room. Within the railing sat six quill-driving gentlemen... all too profoundly immersed in their oriental studies to have any sense of my presence."*

Lamb described office life in his fictional essay *The Superannuated Man.* In his own office life he complained about the long hours, and he was not pleased when a problem at work led him to cancel an annual holiday due to be spent with Coleridge. When the company banned days off for religious feasts, he wrote to his poet friend, *"I have one holiday, which is Christmas day itself, nakedly."* But he was grateful for the steady income: *"Welcome, dead timber of a desk that makes me live. A little grumbling is wholesome medicine for the spleen; but in my inner heart do I improve and embrace this unclose but unharrassing way of life."*

He learned to 'flourish' his handwriting, and worked in the Accountants Office until his retirement, keeping track of warehouse movements and auction sales, though he was one of the best known writers of his day. *"My printed works,"* he said, *"were my recreations; my real works may be found on the shelves in Leadenhall Street, filling some hundred folios."*

Those hundred folios are now among the fourteen kilometres of shelving that the British Library built in Euston for the 70,000 volumes of official publications,

105,000 manuscript and 40,000 maps. The Library acquired them from the Foreign and Commonwealth Offices in 1982 along with the archives of the Board of Control or Board of Commissioners for the Affairs of India (1784–

1858), the India Office (1858–1947) and the Burma Office (1937–48).

In 2000, a couple of years after the new Library building opened, it mounted 'Trading Places: the East India Company and Asia 1800–1834', an exhibition to commemorate the Company's 400th anniversary. Among many documents it could call on were the founding subscription list from 1599 with the names of the first 218 subscribers, and a petition by the young Warren Hastings to the Court of Directors asking for employment, written in a long, sloping hand. The collection contains everything from ships' logs to baptisms and burials, and less than one percent of it lines the walls of the Library's third-floor Asia and Africa Reading Room. The room feels as if it might be in the old India Office in Whitehall, annexed, perhaps, to the Council Chamber. Models of ships that sailed to India are in glass cases, there are busts of Governors-General Warren Hastings and Charles Cornwallis, and high on the wall are full-length portraits in gilt frames of significant figures, including two by Zoffany, and a picture commissioned by the Company of Clive accepting money from the Nawab of Bengal for his fund for disabled soldiers and widows. On the south wall is the Company's golden coat of arms, more than a metre square and looking as fresh as the day it was installed above the Chairman's seat in the Directors' Court Room in 1730. When the goods and chattels from Leadenhall Street went up for auction, this impressive emblem of the mighty Company fetched seven pounds ten shillings.

The Library also has many intriguing scraps among its treasures. A flier dated 1800 from Welch & Stalker, a shop at 134 Leadenhall Street, recommends a hundred or so 'Necessaries for a Writer to India' and sums up the aspirations of the young employee in search of adventure. These include a cot, pistols, Arabian poetry, Persian dictionary, Moorish grammar, wax candles, tobacco, saddle and bridle, travelling-café, all sorts of gadgets and a full wardrobe of suitable clothes.

Through the system of Writers, men such as Sir Stamford Raffles, who had little formal education, not only found good financial prospects but could make their mark in any number of scientific and cultural disciplines. It also offered prospects for atheists and non-conformists whose beliefs barred them from entry to Oxford or Cambridge, though a certificate of baptism in the Anglican church was essential. Applicants had to present a formal petition for employment, offering such promises as behaving *"with the greatest diligence and fidelity"*. Former schoolmasters had to provide testimonials of their mild temper, and a bond was required as surety. In Lamb's case it was £500. He had no salary for the first three years, though there was a small annual gratuity. The rewards came with years of service and a decent pension.

Lamb lived in the era of the Romantics, whose adherents were often seduced by ideas of the Orient. Its leading figures, such as Coleridge and Wordsworth, had friends and relations in the Company. Had young Lord Byron succeeded in making a journey to India, as he had wished, he might have found himself among friends, though few, perhaps, with his burning irredentist ideals. The history and customs of the East were beginning to be discovered and appreciated by the West. Language, archaeology, botany, geology and religion were all subjects of lengthy enquiry. Books and papers started to accumulate at East India House, and after a proposal was made for a public repository for Oriental writing, a library was established in 1800. The first Librarian was Charles Wilkinson, who had begun his career as a printer in Frome, Somerset. At the age of twenty-one he was sent as a Writer to Bengal. There, with the technician Panchanan Karmakar, he cast the first typeface in Bengali, which brought him the title of 'the Caxton of India'. He also made the first translation into English of the Hindu epic *Bhegavade Gita,* a dialogue between the Warrior-Prince Arjuna and the god Krishna disguised as a charioteer. He was one of the first members of the Asiatic Society, a forum for Oriental studies founded by the great linguist Sir William Jones, judge of the supreme court in Calcutta, whose memorial is the only one to be erected by the Company in St Paul's Cathedral.

On the death of Jones, Henry Thomas Colebrooke became President of the Society and he would later set up the Royal Asiatic Society in London. Colebrooke was steeped in the East India Company, which he served for more than three decades. His father, the banker Sir George Colebrooke, had been the Company's Chairman, and

his brother also served in India. Educated at home, Henry was appointed to a Writership in Bengal in 1782, and in 1805 he was made Professor of Hindu Law and Sanskrit at Calcutta's Fort William College, which Richard Wellesley had established for the study of Indian languages, history and law. Colebrooke became the leading British Sanskrit scholar and on his return to England he set up the Royal Asiatic Society at his house at 32 Argyll Street, which is commemorated today with a plaque to Madame de Staël who had stayed there ten years previously. He also co-founded the Royal Astronomical Society, of which he became the second president.

The Royal Asiatic Society is now based in Stephenson's Way, Euston, running workshops and holding talks and seminars in its 100-seat Lecture Hall. Its library has some 80,000 volumes, and it still has a small object collection of paintings, prints and drawings. Its historic museum collection, which included the Ajanta cave paintings, was gradually dispersed as space became a premium, most of it in the 1920s when the majority of items were taken by the V&A and the British Museum, with some ethnographic pieces going to the Horniman Museum in south London.

Cataloguing, keeping records, was just one aspect of the work of the East India Company's essential clerical staff for whom the phrase 'civil servant' was coined. Its methods of recruitment and promotion were to define the civil service in both Britain and India. The founding document for its national establishment was *The Organisation of the Permanent Civil Service*, commissioned by the British government and published in 1854. Its co-author was Charles Trevelyan, who had spent a dozen years in India for the Company acquiring the habits and practice that were the basis for the report. These stipulated that entrance should be by examination, that applicants should have a good all-round knowledge to allow employees to be transferred between departments, that promotion should be on the grounds of merit only and there would be a strict structure of grades. These ideas were taken up throughout the Commonwealth and still hold good today among Britain's civil service staff of half a million, 50,000 of whom work in the Foreign and Commonwealth Office.

After the demise of the Company, Trevelyan became Governor of Madras and, from 1862 to 1865, Indian Finance Minister. He was from Taunton, Somerset, the son of an Archdeacon, and he was a product of the East India College at Haileybury in Hertfordshire. The college had started life in 1806, half a dozen years after the Addiscombe Military Seminary had

opened. For three years it operated out of Hertford Castle, a mansion that had been occupied by several Company men, now the local council offices. Hertford is at the head of the Lee Navigation canal, some thirty miles from London on the way to Cambridge. A more suitably grand college was meanwhile being built a couple of miles away on Hertford Heath. Designed by William Wilkins, architect of the National Gallery, the majestic neo-classical lines have a familiar portico and dome. Haileybury later became the Imperial Service College and is now a co-educational private school the size of a small town where 500 of the 750 pupils are boarders paying £10,000 a term.

Opposite the school is The College Arms, a well-kept, unostentatious Grade II listed pub with a large garden. When the college arrived, this small ale house was expanded to provide accommodation. On

its walls are old pictures of Wilkins' school building and maps of India and Asia. It is fully modernised, with a restaurant and quiz nights, and despite its obvious awareness of its legacy, some

imagination is needed to think of Company men and boys at leisure in this building that many of them would have known well.

Writerships in the Company's overseas civil service were nominated by the Directors, and graduates from Haileybury would become administrators in Asia and in Cape Town. Trevelyan had been taught at Haileybury by the Reverend Robert Malthus, the college's Professor of History and Political Economy, whose *Essay on the Principal of Population* put forward the theory that when populations reached the limit of the food supply, poverty and starvation were inevitable, and that famine and disease were natural or divine interventions to prevent overpopulation. His pupils called him 'pop' for population, and the Malthusian theories affected the Company's attitude towards the periodic famines in India, which claimed millions of lives. It was bad luck for the Irish, too, that Trevelyan was Assistant Secretary to HM Treasury during the Great Famine.

The other influential 19th-century philosopher associated with the Company was John Stuart Mill, who believed that in a civilised society the only legitimate reason for exercising power over anybody against his or her will was to prevent harm to others, and his works address the complex issues of how to live in a free society that remain at the heart of liberal thinking. Mill arrived at East India House in 1823. His father, the Scottish historian and political theorist James Mill, had been appointed Assistant Examiner of Indian Correspondence four years earlier, following the publication of the ten-volume *History of British India*. Although happy to admit that he had never visited India, James Mill believed his views were more objective for staying at home, from where he wrote what is, to the modern reader, breathtakingly sweeping descriptions of Asian people. Of Hindus and Chinese, he wrote, "*Both nations are to nearly an equal degree tainted with the vices of insincerity; dissembling, treacherous, mendacious, to an excess which surpasses even the usual measure of uncultivated society. Both are disposed to excessive exaggeration with regard to everything relating to themselves. Both are cowardly and unfeeling. Both are in the highest degree conceited of themselves, and full of affected contempt for others. Both are, in the physical sense, disgustingly unclean in their persons and houses.*"

This was not the considered, sympathetic voice of Warren Hastings or the members of the Asiatic Society, and it would set a tone for the Raj that was to come. James Mill was, however, a good friend of the social reformer and utilitarian Jeremy Bentham who was a godfather to John Stuart, and Bentham rented him a house in Queen Anne's Gate where he wrote his Indian treatise. Mill junior's own writings had little to do with India but they did express the belief that 'barbaric' people should be educated before they were capable of self-government. Schooled at home with terrifying vigour by his father, John Stuart started as a Writer at the age of seventeen in 1823, working for his father who was by then Chief Examiner. One of the most important offices in Leadenhall Street, it oversaw the Political, Revenue, Public and Judicial branches of the Company and was a conduit for policy documents between the Board of Directors and the Governor-General in India.

After Mill's death in 1836 there was a twenty-year interregnum when Thomas Love Peacock, the poet and friend of Shelley, was Chief Examiner. Even less well known today than Lamb, despite his memorable name, Dorset-born Peacock wrote poetry and novels successfully, and was also in the forefront of developing iron steamers for the Company. On his departure, John Stuart became the Company's last Chief Examiner. The post included the role of spokesman, and shortly after his appointment, following the Indian Mutiny, he was instructed by the Directors to compose a defence of the Company to put before Parliament, which was about to end its activities. It was a cause he felt strongly about, not wanting the administration of India to fall into the hands of the *"folly and mischief"* of Parliament. His cause was unsuccessful and he declined a position on the government's subsequent India Council.

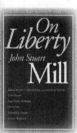

During his thirty-five-year career at East India House John Stuart Mill penned almost two thousand dispatches, and in his own time had spent the last few years of his Company career writing his best known work, *On Liberty*. Like Charles Lamb, he was not only able to produce his own work, but he also found employment at East India House conducive to his projects. In his autobiography, he wrote:

"I do not know any one of the occupations by which a subsistence can now be gained, more suitable than such as this to anyone who, not being in independent circumstances, desires to devote a part of the twenty-four hours to private intellectual pursuits... I have, through life, found office duties an actual rest from the other occupations which I have carried on simultaneously with them. They were sufficiently intellectual not to be a distasteful drudgery without being such as to cause any strain upon the mental powers of a person used to abstract thought or the labour of careful literary composition."

CHAPLAINS

A woman in a colourful sari beneath a light coat greets visitors to Nicholas Hawksmoor's Christ Church in Spitalfields. She is quite at home in this echoing space, which she has known through its comprehensive restoration completed in 2004, ten years after she began working as an East End missionary, bringing Christianity to the benighted heathens of London. She also helps to keep discussion and information flowing between faiths, particularly the Muslim community  of Bengalis from what is now Bangladesh and north-east India, of which there are some 50,000 in Spitalfields, and two-thirds of the population in the whole borough of Tower Hamlets.

It was once Europeans who took their missionary zeal to India, so it seems a curious reversal. Back home in Kolkata, she says, Christians have been finding life increasingly difficult under a more fundamentalist Indian government. Hindus and Christians have always got on, and Muslims, too, though there has long been a fanatical element. But now the ruling Hindus are becoming intolerant. The Christian community she and her father belong to in the capital of the state of West Bengal has rooms in a building that is topped with a cross, and they have been told they must remove it.

"A cross is now seen as something from the Raj, not something from the Christian church," she says. "They say it is pro-British, but I tell them that Christ gave his life for the whole world." She makes a sweeping gesture that encompasses a huge, imaginary globe. "Not just for Christians, but for everybody."

The East India Company was not in the business of spreading the Christian faith, and until its charter was renewed with a 'pious clause' in 1813, it managed to resist all attempts by parliamentarians and evangelicals to force it to become involved with missionaries. The Company did, however, adopt a policy of recruiting a Chaplain on board any vessel that either had a crew of more than a hundred men, or on a vessel of more than 500 tons. There are stories of crew numbers put at ninety-nine men and a boy, and of vessels registered at 499 tons to escape the decree.

The Company's lack of support did not mean that English missionaries could not find their own way there. The first recorded was Father Thomas Stephens, the son of a Wiltshire merchant, who began his work in Goa eighty years before the Company was

formed, and both Catholic and Protestant European countries had early missions. But Company men needed God on their side. Half of the men and women who set off for India never returned to Britain and of the 665 Chaplains who sailed east with the Company over the course of 258 years, 210 died in service. The perils of sea voyages were enough to put the fear of God into any mariner, whose superstitions were anyway legendary. Company ships always had a Bible on board, daily prayers were read from the *Book of Common Prayer*, and from 1609 Chaplains sailing on Company ships and taking up posts in forts and factories were chosen from recommendations of local City churches. These included St Helen's and St Andrew Undershaft, both now overshadowed by 'the Gherkin' in St Mary Axe. The Chaplains were a mixed bunch, invariably graduates of Oxford and Cambridge and friends of Directors. Until 1698 they were whittled down for selection by sermons at these churches based on texts either of their own choice  or supplied by the Company. After 1638 the Bishop of London and the Archbishop of Canterbury were involved in the selection, and it became Company policy for all garrisons and factories to establish a place of worship.

An early convert was 'Peter' or 'Pope Peter', a lad from Masulipatan on the Coromandel coast in the Bay of Bengal where the Company had established its earliest factory. Arriving in London on the Company's tenth returning voyage, he was the first Indian ever known to set foot in Britain. Eager and bright, he had been handed over by a Dutch East India captain and put in the care of the fleet's Chaplain, Patrick Copland, a Presbyterian from Aberdeen. Hoping that he would be converted and return to India to preach among his own, the Company paid for two years' education in England during which he learned 'Roman' and 'Secretary' (Latin and English) and studied the Bible. It was

James I who decreed that the young Indian should be christened with the name of Peter. No record exists of his real name. His education considered complete, with the Archbishop of Canterbury's blessing he was baptised in St Dionis Backchurch in Lime Street, near East India House, by Dr Wood, Rector of St Helen's, on December 22, 1614. The occasion was highly publicised and the ceremony, which took place in front of East India Company Directors and the Lord Mayor of London, attracted huge crowds wanting to glimpse in the wintery light a lad from a land of colour and sun.

Less than two years after Peter's baptism, another 'Indian' came to excite Londoners' imaginations. Princess Pocahontas and her entourage of Powhatan natives arrived from Virginia to the delight of James I and the court, but there is no memorial in the city to either of these historic events, though

Pocahontas is remembered in Gravesend (see page 200.) All that is known of Peter subsequently is that he did go to India. A couple of letters signed '*Petrus Papa*' were sent to Copland, who by then had sailed to Virginia to continue his mission and establish the East India School in America, funded, he hoped, by the Company. But the school building was burnt to the ground in a massacre in 1621 and was not replaced.

Dionis Backchurch was demolished in 1878, its marble baptismal font going to a new St Dionis in Parsons Green in West London, built on the proceeds of the sale of the site. There it sits in a corner with a wonderful hood depicting the previous church, rebuilt after the Great Fire. But without an overhead pulley to raise it, the font is too impractical for regular use, and a portable vessel makes do for baptisms.

St Helen's in Bishopsgate and St Andrew Undershaft are rare medieval survivors, St Andrew now acting as the church hall for St Helen's, a former nunnery church and the largest in the City. Abutting property held by East India House it benefitted from gifts and legacies from Company men, and tea sales were once held in its churchyard. In London only Westminster Abbey has more memorials, yet among the many tombs and plaques there is little evidence of the East India  Company. There is a kneeler monument of one of the Company's original subscribers, Richard Staper, and a plaque to James Cruickshank Grant, a Lieutenant-Colonel in the Bengal Army. After the Bishopsgate bombs planted by the IRA in 1992 and 1993, it was redesigned by the architect Quinlan Terry, who altered its axis and took its floor down to its medieval level. Before that, it was possible to see the fading letters on a marble tablet in the chancel floor commemorating a Company director, Thomas Mun. Born half a mile away, Mun was a staunch defender of the Company's practice of exporting silver bullion to buy goods in Asia, publishing in 1621 *A Discourse of Trade, from England unto the East Indies; answering to diverse Objections which are usually made against the same.* This was the first written work to recognise the importance of the balance of trade.

SHIPS & SHIPPING

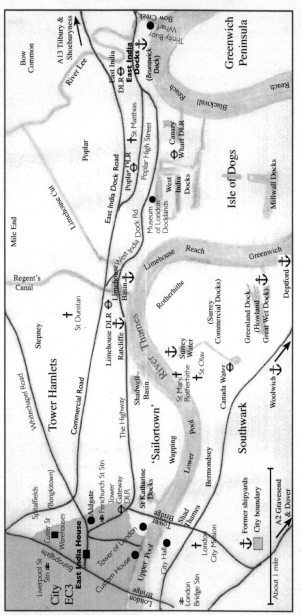

SHIPS

It is difficult to imagine a Britain in which most of its trade is controlled by a monopoly of a single trucking company. Yet that is what the East India Company essentially was, except instead of trucks it had ships. In the 233 years between its inauguration and its loss of monopoly rights in 1833, its three-masted wooden leviathans undertook 4,600 voyages,  importing millions of tons of goods into Britain.

Built on the Thames at Deptford, Blackwall, Rotherhithe, Limehouse and Northfleet, these were the largest cargo carriers in the world. Each one might require 3,000 fully grown oak trees, seventy-four tons of cordage and 21,000 yards of canvas, yet they generally completed no more than half a dozen round trips. By the 19th century, a ship of 1,400 net tons could accommodate, at a pinch, six hundred. Crews of 120 to 150 might be outnumbered by soldiers and marines, all sleeping in hammocks slung at as little as fourteen-inch intervals, while passengers or 'landsmen', if lucky, had the relative comforts of cabins temporarily partitioned in the roundhouse beneath the poop deck. Well-armed, with two and sometimes three gun-decks, they could be mistaken for men-of-war. Given a government 'Letter of Marque and Reprisal' they were at liberty to attack 'pirates' and capture prize ships from any deemed enemy, although they were under strict instructions to avoid conflict where possible. 'Stern chasers' were installed to discourage unwanted pursuers. Within ten days of his return, a ship's captain had to deliver four copies of his log to the Company, adding observations and navigational comments.

Initially, naval ships were bought and converted. *Red Dragon*, the ship that Sir James Lancaster commanded on the Company's first voyage after chasing silver on the Spanish Main, had been built in 1595 at London's first royal dockyard, the King's Yard in Deptford just upriver from the royal palace at Greenwich. On the outside curve of the great meander of Greenwich Reach that loops around the Isle of Dogs, the riverbed at Deptford was scoured free of silt. It is still deep enough to provide anchorage

for ships as large as the 21,550-ton helicopter carrier HMS *Ocean*, which has a twenty-one-foot draught.

For more than two centuries Deptford was synonymous with the King's Navy, and it was a focus of national events. Founded by Henry VIII in 1513, the Royal Dockyard had launched the *Mary Rose* and was associated with Elizabethan buccaneers. Londoners had flocked here to see the Queen knight Francis Drake on board the *Golden Hinde* after his epic round-the-world voyage that brought the royal coffers substantial Spanish booty. The galleon became London's first historic museum ship, and today a replica can be boarded at St Mary Overie Dock in Southwark.

The Company's initial voyages proved so lucrative that it decided to build its own vessels beside the

King's Yard, at Deptford Green by the mouth of the Ravensbourne, so it could share facilities, labour and expertise. The first Company-built East Indiamen here were *Trades Increase* and *Peppercorn*,
launched in 1610, and soon the yard was employing some 500 carpenters, joiners, caulkers, ropemakers, anchor smiths and other craftsmen.

When more space was needed, the Company chose a site closer to the City on the north bank at Blackwall by Bow Creek on the River Lea. Like Deptford, Blackwall was on the faster-flowing bank of the river as it strikes north around the Isle of Dogs. The Company's first buildings occupied what was initially called the East India Yard in 1612. Within two decades it was one of London's biggest employers, with more than 400 in its workforce. It had four dry docks, including a 300-foot double dry dock that could accommodate two East Indiamen at a time.

Riches from the East were, however, patchy, not helped by either the Anglo-Dutch conflicts or the English Civil War. No longer willing to have the expense of maintaining the yards, the Company soon retired from any direct involvement in the shipbuilding business, but it kept a base in Deptford where its workshops, iron foundries, gunpowder house and stores had grown around an area called Stowage, remembered in the street of the same name that runs beside the ancient church of St Nicholas where many shipbuilders are buried.

Although the Company sold its Deptford shipyard in 1644 and Blackwall in 1667, its East Indiamen continued to be built in both places, as well as in other commercial shipyards that were growing up along the Thames. These businesses were in the hands of a few well-known families, and their tangle of intermarriages and partnerships makes their connections a paper chase. There were the Bronsdens and Dudmans in Deptford, and the Barnards, too, who were at Rotherhithe, as were the Wells, while the Johnsons had taken over the Blackwall yard. These names crop up in Company records not only as builders and 'husbands' of East Indiamen, but as Directors and even as ships' Commanders.

'Husbands' or 'husbandmen' was the name given to the backers who chartered the ships, after whom some were named. Having adopted a vessel, they would find investors to take shares in the voyages, which were usually divided into sixteenths. However, it was down to the Company to appoint and dismiss Commanders, who remained fully responsible to the Directors in Leadenhall Street. Usually gentlemen, Commanders could expect to become rich through trading on their own account, taking a limited number of goods to Asia and trading port-to-port. It is a sign of the potential profits that could be made by officers that some might invest several thousand pounds to secure a position, but after reforms in 1799, the sale of commands was outlawed. In addition, after swearing an oath of allegiance Commanders had to deposit with the Company a large penalty bond, and on their return from each voyage had to pay a fee.

Master shipwrights could also have a financial interest in the ships that they built and maintained, as would sailmakers, victuallers and others essential to their construction. John Perry had an interest in Company ships. After buying the Blackwall Yard from the Johnsons, he made Blackwall the biggest business on the Thames when he created the Brunswick Dock on its eastern side in 1790. Although it was named in honour of George III, it was commonly known as Mr Perry's Dock. It was built to deal with Company ships and could refit and provision thirty at a time, and thirty lesser ships more. For many years its 120-foot brick-and-timber mast house, designed for East Indiamen, was a landmark on the river. Although a main mast could weigh fifteen tons, it was able to raise the spars on a three-masted ship in a fraction of the time it had previously taken.

The Perrys were followed by the Wigrams, who were directors of the Company and invested heavily in East Indiamen, and the Greens, who saw the formation of the East India Dock Company, described in the Shipping chapter (page 176). Perry had an interest in Howland Great Wet Dock where East Indiamen continued to be fitted out. It had been leased from Josiah Child's granddaughter Elizabeth Howland by the Wells brothers and was the oldest wet dock on the Thames' south bank. It also offered a safe haven for shipping and has

survived as Greenland Dock, the largest body of water in Rotherhithe, though now around half its original size.

In Limehouse, where the oak hull of the East Indiaman *Canton* was sunk into a former mast pond to create a dry dock that lasted seventy years, the Batsons were a prominent name. In Northfleet, where thirty-five East Indiamen were launched, the Pitchers were the master builders.

Commercial yards built both merchant and naval warships, and paintings from the 18th century show East Indiamen with Company crests on their gilded

transom sterns in a flutter of pennants and flags fit for a monarch or at the least an Admiral of the Fleet. In her 1981 book, *Lords of the Seas*, the historian Jean Sutton wrote, *"Considering the fact that Indiamen and naval ships were built side by side in the same yards, by the same men, under similar stringent conditions, it is surprising that the Company's ships were superior in many ways."*

Armaments came from a variety of sources. First it was the Royal Arsenal in the Tower of London, to which the company was contracted to supply Indian saltpetre for gunpowder. Woolwich, which became a royal dockyard in Queen Elizabeth's reign, was another source. This was where every cannon, whatever its origin, had to be 'proofed' ot tested before the start of each voyage.

Ships would traditionally return to their birthplace for overhauling and refitting. Hulls needed scraping clean of barnacles, worm-eaten timbers had to be replaced, and there was re-caulking and re-trenailing – renewing the pegs that held the planks. After copper plates had been introduced to protect the hulls and increase the ships' speed, hulls needed re-coppering, too.

Shipwrights were freelance operators who owned their own tools and worked in small teams. A peripatetic bunch, they never had a long-term home for their guild. Those working on seagoing vessels

downriver of London Bridge were known as Foreign Shipwrights, and they set up their own Hall for '*The Shipwrights of Redriff* (Rotherhithe) *in the County of*

Surrey'. Freemen in the City who operated around Thames Street had their own organisation, though many were compelled to abandon their tar- and timber-filled yards in the wake of the Great Fire. Even after the two sides had united under a Livery granted in 1782, they lived like hermit crabs in other Liveries' halls. Today the Worshipful Company of Shipwrights inhabits the Ironmongers Hall behind the Museum of London, and there is no sign of the yards where their forebears worked.

The once busy waterfront between Deptford and Greenwich has been developed. Apartments rise above the sludgy bed of the Ravensbourne where at low tide visitors to the Creekside Centre put on waders to go mudlarking for old workers' tools and crabs, hoping to glimpse a black redstart, which they have made their emblem. The King's Yard lies beneath Convoys Wharf. It was last active importing newsprint for Rupert Murdoch's publications. The majestic 1840s Olympia building covering two slipways that faced the now filled-in basin have been listed, and in 2011, after the Wharf had remained disused for fourteen years, the Museum of London Archaeology (MOLA) uncovered evidence of the docks, mast ponds and a Tudor storehouse before backfilling the site for development. Two riverside survivors are the Master Shipwright's House, built in 1708 by the Navy Board and now privately owned, and a row of Georgian buildings from the Navy's 35-acre Victualling Yard, now the Pepys Estate. Other vestiges of Deptford's naval past have recently disappeared. The Dockyard's Storehouse Clocktower, dubbed Nelson's Clock, was moved by the GLC in 1991 to the new town of Thamesmead where it stands without explanation in the midst of the shopping centre. In 2013 Lewisham Council removed the large anchor in Deptford High Street that had been donated by Chatham Dockyard because it attracted drinkers. One symbol that does remain is Deptford's 1905 Town Hall, now used by

Goldsmith's College. On its facade lofty statues of Drake, Blake and Nelson look out over the traffic of New Cross Road, while high above them floats a golden galleon weathervane, and when the wind is in the south-west, it points to where the dockyards once flourished, barely a mile away.

Shipbuilding skills may have been lost in London, but should they return there is plenty of material to draw on. In 1706 the Navy Board decreed that models as well as plans should be made for all new ships and some of these are among the collection of 3,500 models held by the National Maritime Museum. It was a lack of plans that proved a challenge in Sweden when it came to building the full-scale replica of the East Indiaman *Götheborg*. The original was launched in 1739, just eight years after the Swedish East India Company was established, and she made three journeys to China before hitting a rock in 1745 just outside her home port of Gothenburg. It wasn't until divers located the wreck in 1984 that enthusiasts could think about building a replica, based on what they found. It took some time to work out her construction and she took eleven years to complete.

Contemporaneous with the *Götheborg* was the *Somerset*, the earliest East Indiaman in the NMM's collection, made *"in the style of the Navy Board models, though with some anomalies and built to a slightly lower standard"*, and now in the Traders Gallery. The bulk of the museum's collection, however, is in a vast temperature-controlled pod in the Smithery at the former Royal Navy Dockyard at Chatham. With a famous ropery, mould loft, steam chest, anchor pit and other vestiges from its glory days, as well as the 19th-century barque-rigged sloop HMS *Gannet*, the Historic Dockyard is now run by Chatham Historic Dockyards Trust and is a working dockyard. Beside the River Medway as it starts to open out towards the Thames, an hour's train ride from Charing Cross, this is a place to visit to see how wooden ships were built.

In 2001 a model of the East Indiaman *Falmouth*, with a cutaway side, was commissioned for the new Museum of London in Docklands. This heavily armed, 36-gun East Indiaman was built by Perrys at Blackwall Yard in 1752, and the replica was constructed by Alan Berry-Robinson, who has a model-making business in Sussex. Made entirely of timber, principally lemonwood from South America, *Falmouth* took nine months to complete, based on drawings of the vessel in the archives of the National Maritime Museum. Its crew wear colourful seamen's

clothes and its holds are crammed with cargo from the East, based on the ship's log of her only voyage to Canton. Some of the miniature jar containers, says Berry-Robinson, who is a naval historian as well as a model maker, proved particularly taxing.

Amateur enthusiasts can buy model boat kits from The Dockyard Model Shop in Chatham, a ships' chandlers in miniature, run by Robert Bright who has been making model boats for forty years. A 1:75 model kit of the *Falmouth* with a five-star 'difficulty' rating is otherwise available from Euromodels of Como in Italy for 646 euros.

Real East Indiamen were seldom built abroad but many British-owned 'country' ships that traded among Asian ports came from local yards. They had the benefit of hardwoods, mainly teak, which gave them a much longer life, but London shipbuilders had a monopoly, and there were always protests whenever it was mooted that vessels could be built overseas, with the added grumble that nobody could match British craftsmanship. During the Napoleonic Wars when commercial yards were fully occupied building ships for the Navy, a 'timber crisis' was blamed in part on the huge East Indiamen. It was then that Jamsetjee Bomanjee, father of a shipbuilding dynasty at the Bombay Dockyard, stepped into the breach, carrying out commissions both for the Company and for the Royal Navy. A portrait of him with a silver ruler in his belt, a gift from the grateful Navy, hangs in the Maritime Museum in Greenwich. Proof of the longevity of these Indian teak-timbered ships can be seen in Hartlepool where HMS *Tricomelee* is a main attraction in the Maritime Experience. Built in the Bombay dockyards in 1817 by the Wadia

family firm, which is still in business, she is the oldest British warship afloat.

Another long-lived Wadia ship was the *Cornwallis*, the largest sailing warship in the Greenwich museum's model collection. Launched in Bombay in 1813, she was one of several ships designed for the Company that ended up in the Royal Navy's hands. The Treaty of Nanking that concluded the First Opium War was signed on board, and she did service in the Crimean War, ending her days as a jetty in Sheerness. Even then she proved remarkably resilient, and in 1957 when her 144-year-old hull was deemed obstructive, explosives had to be used to remove it. HMS *Wellesley*, ordered by the Company and launched in Bombay in 1812, was another hand-me-down for the Royal Navy and another great survivor, seeing action in Crimea and living long enough to be bombed to bits in the Thames in the Second World War. Some of her timbers are said to have been used for the postwar reconstruction of the Royal Courts of Justice in the Strand.

The perils of journeying east lay not just in unknown foreign waters. Dangers started close to home. One of the problems was that in order to harness the Trade and Monsoon winds that would take ships across the Atlantic and Indian oceans via the Company's island of St Helena and the Cape of Good Hope, they had to leave London in winter, and January proved to be the cruellest month. A number of ships either did not get far, or they foundered at the end of the following year

on the last few miles home. The outbound *Albion* had been wrecked on Long Sand Head in the Thames Estuary on January 7, 1765 with forty-seven chests of silver, coin and plate, 884 lead ingots and a consignment of coloured glass ingots but no loss of life. The wreck was found in 1985 and some items were exhibited in Ramsgate Maritime Museum.

On January 6, 1786 the *Halsewell* went down in a snowstorm off the Isle of Purbeck. Of the 240 crew and passengers, including a contingent of soldiers on their way to Madras, only seventy-four survived. Captain Pierce, the oldest master mariner in the Company fleet, who was on the point of retiring, perished along with his two daughters.

Another family tragedy that tugged at the nation's heart was the loss in 1805 of the *Earl of Abergavenny* under the command of John Wordsworth, younger brother of the poet William. The family had invested heavily in the trip, with the hope that it might improve the fortunes of William, who had not long been married to Mary and was living in tiny Dove Cottage with their first child and his sister Dorothy. The *Abergavenny* was built at Pitchers Yard in Northfleet and this was her fifth trip east. She had a crew of around 180, thirty-four guns and had seen action at the Battle of Pulo Aura. A cargo of silver to the tune of £70,000 went with the hope of trading in Bengal and China. Commander John Wordsworth had brought along a number of items for private trade, though he had previously been fined by the Company for dealing in camlet (a woven cloth), which was forbidden. In a letter to Dorothy he complained that he had been the first officer to be fined for something he believed had become common practice. It is a small irony that the Company had by this time begun exporting Indian-grown opium to China, where the drug was banned. John's brother, William, would later fall out with his fellow poet Samuel Taylor Coleridge on account of Coleridge's opium habit.

Travelling in the annual convoy of East Indiamen from Gravesend, *Abergavenny* first hit trouble in the Downs, when she collided with the *Warren Hastings* in a storm. The *Warren Hastings* was so badly damaged that she had to return for repairs, missing the season. The remaining five East Indiamen continued to Portsmouth, an embarcation port for passengers and troops. *Abergavenny* took on 108 soldiers from the King's army as well as EIC officers and cadets, including Joseph Wordsworth, the son of another John Wordsworth, cousin of the incumbent captain. It was a local pilot that they took on board who managed to drive them on to the Shambles Rock, where the ship sank on the freezing night of February 5. John Wordsworth was among the 261 'crew, soldiers, Chinamen and some Portuguese' who perished, though young Joseph, sent in a small boat to fetch help, survived.

The largest East Indiaman to go down in home waters was the 1,249-ton *Hindostan*, driven onto Wedge Sands, off Margate, on January 11, 1803. Her pumps jammed with sand, she broke her back and two dozen lives were lost. There were thirteen cases of bullion on board, and Company agents salvaged what they could.

On the night of January 25, 1809, a fleet of three ships, the *Admiral Gardner, Britannia* and *Apollo* all went down in bad weather as they sailed out of the Thames Estuary into the North Sea heading for the Dover Straits and Madras. Unable to prevent their anchors dragging in the storm, they were blown onto Goodwin Sands where they sank. This was to have been the third journey to Asia for the Rotherhithe-built *Admiral Gardner*. Among her cargo was forty-six tons of East India Company copper coins, minted at Matthew Boulton's Soho Works, to be paid to Indian workers who could only use them in Company stores. In 1976, these started to appear during dredging, and eight years later a salvage operation recovered a million coins from what is now a protected wreck site. The *Ogle Castle* was another victim of Goodwin Sands. Returning from India with a cargo of cotton she sank on November 3, 1825 with the loss of all hands.

There were plenty of perils and adventures on the high seas, too. Looking for an alternative route to the East, in 1782 the Company sent a secret mission to China via Cape Horn. The Commander of the packet *Antelope* was Henry Wilson from Rotherhithe, and his son and brother sailed with him. They reached China safely, but on the return trip came to grief on the Pelau islands, to the east of the Philippines, where the ship ran aground and broke up. A crew member from Macau was able to speak with the locals, and the English muskets were particularly welcome when their host, the *rupack*, or king, Abba Thulle, needed to deal with a rival. The king was also greatly impressed at the way the Company men went about cannibalising the wreck to build a new ship, and he asked for his second son, Prince Lee Boo, to go to England to learn their skills. So they all set sail on the new vessel for China, where they picked up another ship, the *Morse*. Arriving in England, the prince lived for just a few months in Wilson's household in Paradise Row in Rotherhithe before catching smallpox. He was twenty years old, and he is buried in St Mary's Rotherhithe, one of London's most evocative maritime churches, which stands next to the Mayflower pub from where the Pilgrim Fathers' ship set sail.

Prince Lee Boo was interred in Captain Wilson's family tomb in the graveyard, and the words on its lid read: "*This stone is inscribed by the Honourable East India Company as a testimony of the Esteem for the humane and kind treatment afforded by his Father to Captain Wilson and the Crew of the Ship the Antelope which was wrecked off that island on the night of the 9th August 1783. Stop reader stop. Let Nature claim a tear, a prince of mine, Lee Boo, lies buried here.*"

Seasonal voyages died out with the coming of steam. No longer did ships have to leave in January, and arrival times could be scheduled. Britain's first iron warship was the *Nemesis*, a paddle steamer with sails commissioned by the Secret Committee of the East India Company for the First Opium War. Although Wigram and Green began building small steamships at Blackwall in 1821, *Nemesis* came off the slips in the Mersey at Birkenhead eighteen years later. She was the first steamship to round the Cape of Good Hope, and she arrived in China in time to be extremely useful in the taking of Canton.

After the Company had lost its monopoly over both the India and China trades, it continued to administer the territories under its control. Faster ships known as Blackwall Frigates, designed like naval frigates with single gun decks, replaced traditional Indiamen and offered passengers comfort as well as speed. In addition to carrying cargoes, they had to compete with the new passenger and mail services offered by the likes of the Peninsular and Oriental Steam Navigation Company, P&O. The first Blackwall Frigate to make the China run was the 871-ton *Seringapatam* in 1837. Another *Seringapatam* was built for the Navy at Bombay Dockyard ten years later and its highly fanciful figurehead is now in the National Maritime Museum. Given the ship's name, it was often imagined that the turbanned character astride a bird beneath an umbrella was Tipu Sultan, who was mythologised long after his death.

As competition from other British yards and from abroad increased, and with trade monopolies ended, the emphasis was on speed, which merchant clippers began to provide. On December 3, 1850 the American ship *Oriental*, developed from the Baltimore Clipper design, came sailing up the Thames with 1,600 tons of tea, ninety-seven days after leaving Hong Kong, a third of the time it took a laden East Indiamen. For a couple of decades clippers would become the stars of the Asia voyages. In his 1935 book, *The Opium Clippers*, the maritime historian Basil Lubbock summed up the thrill of the days of sail when the Company, short of money but too big to fail, was dragged into the dreadful Opium Wars, growing the drug in India and shipping it illegally into China, where millions became addicted.

"*What more could a merchant adventurer ask for than a trade whose profits were often five hundred or even a thousand fold?*" he asks in a chapter titled 'The Romance of the Opium Trade'. "*Who would not jump out of his soft bed and sling his hammock aboard an opium clipper?*"

It may not have been a drug, but tea still offered

good returns, and it was for the tea trade that the *Cutty Sark*, icon of the Royal Borough of Greenwich, was built. In spite of the undoubted advantages of steam, the *Cutty Sark* was ordered by John Willis, a son of the founder of John Willis & Sons shipping line. He had his first command at the age of nineteen, and came to believe that sail would continue to be more profitable than steam, as the wind provided free energy and valuable cargo space would not be taken up by coal or engine machinery. An inspiration for the *Cutty Sark*'s design came from *The Tweed*, adapted from a paddle steamer built in 1854 by Cursetjee Rustomjee in Bombay, which Willis picked up on the Company's demise and converted to sail. His faith was not misplaced. Built in Dumbarton and running out of East India Docks, the *Cutty Sark* could carry 10,000 chests of China tea, today given a value of more than £18 million. She made eight successful voyages to China before turning her attention to the Australian wool trade.

Cutty Sark was launched in December 22, 1869, five days after the Suez Canal opened, shortening the route to China by 3,000 miles. But the Mediterranean and canals were no place for tall ships. The East India Company had not lived quite long enough to witness the great days of sail drawing to a close.

AMSTERDAM

Among the maritime memorabilia on the quayside at St Katharine Docks is a large anchor with a hefty wooden stock that belonged to the East Indiaman *Amsterdam*. The ship was built not for the Honourable EIC but for VOC (Vereenigde Oostindische Compagnie), the Dutch East India Company, and its last few timbers can occasionally be seen on the beach seventy miles away in Hastings. On spring tides, when the green waters of the English Channel roll away towards France, a few stumps of the *Amsterdam* are revealed, stuck in the clay like rotten teeth among the ancient trunks and boles of a petrified forest to which they seem so completely to belong.

Built in Amsterdam to the designs of Charles Bentham, an English shipwright working for the Dutch admiralty, she was forty-three metres long and armed with twenty twelve-inch cannons. Her maiden journey had been hard going from the start. Having taken on a cargo of ballast, cannons, wine, textiles, silver and coinage on the island of Texel along with five other vessels bound for the main VOC Dutch East Indies trading port of Batavia (Jakarta), she first attempted to leave home waters in mid-November, 1748. Nearly three months later, on her third attempt to make it out of the wintery North Sea and down the English Channel to the Atlantic, storms worsened. As the ship pitched and rolled, portholes were closed against the crashing waves, and the stench of disease and dysentery, known to English sailors as 'the flux', became unbearable. On board were five passengers, including a VOC merchant, Andries van Bockom, his bride and sister-in-law, 128 soldiers and a crew of 204, only half of whom were expected to survive the round trip. But fever spread and death came early. By the time *Amsterdam* lost her rudder on a sandbank off Pevensey Bay some fifty fatalities had been hastily sewn up in their hammocks and cast into the sea. A similar number looked as if they would soon expire. With little strength to steer the ship by her sails, the enfeebled crew fortified themselves by breaking into the wine cellars. Mutiny threatened, and the thirty-three-year-old captain, William Klump, took the decision to beach the ship at Bulverhythe, in what is now St Leonards-on-Sea, where she broke up, and a year later was declared a total loss. Klump was cleared of all blame, and later made another trip to Batavia.

In 1969 the wreck of the *Amsterdam* was located by archaeologists who declared it to be the most complete surviving example of an East Indiaman, and English Heritage took it into its care. Protected by layers of clay and sand, some cargo had escaped plundering, and a few coins and other small items are now in Hastings' seafront Shipwreck Museum. More remarkably, a celebration dinner was organised in the Netherlands for wine producers from Bergerac to sample the 250-year-old Monbazillac wine found in two hundred large flagons. It was judged 'sublime'.

Plans to take *Amsterdam*'s bare bones back to the

city of her birth did not materialise, but, based on the few remains, a replica of the ship was built over five years from 1985 by volunteers using original materials and tools. Today she lies alongside the city's National Maritime Museum where visitors can have an idea of what it must have been like to be cooped up with 350 men and a cargo of goods to be traded for spices.

Unlike London, where there is no triumphant waving of Company colours, the VOC flag at the stern of the *Amsterdam* flutters with some pride. All great nations have to wrestle with the dual emotions of pride in conquest and shame in the destruction they have wrought, but perhaps because the VOC expired before the rapacious European empire-building of the 19th century, it is more distant in the public consciousness.

Dutch venturers set sail for Asia two years before the first East India Company voyage, and shortly afterwards the VOC was formed by the Netherlands' seafaring towns. The company became hugely successful, soon accounting for more than half the world's shipping and funding a Golden Age. Canalside mansions were built on its fortunes, and several towns have a Peperstraat. Exotic imports crossed the North Sea to England bringing Japanese porcelain and numerous new plants, which arrived along with a taste for all things Dutch with the accession in 1689 of William III, the Stadtholder of the Dutch Republic, and his co-regent, James II's daughter, Mary Stuart. Mary was already famous for the gardens at Het Loo, the couple's palace ninety kilometres east of Amsterdam, which she filled with wonderful plants brought to Europe by the VOC from their Cape Colony in South Africa as well as from Asia. At their new palace at Hampton Court, which Wren was rebuilding, she filled the garden with more than 2,000 exotic species, largely provided by the VOC. 'Stove' houses built by a Dutch carpenter in the South Garden were among the first greenhouses in England, while two large orangeries were filled with the country's biggest citrus collection, celebrating

the lineage of her husband, from the House of Orange-Nassau. The gardens have not survived, but in the 1980s Het Loo was re-laid out and turned into a museum, and in the 1990s 'Queen Mary's Exotick Collection' was reintroduced at Hampton Court.

The VOC was not without its critics, and by the time it was declared bankrupt in 1799, people were saying that the initials VOC stood for *Vergaan Onder Corruptie* ('perished by corruption'). In spite of this familiar story, the company is still part of the Netherlands landscape, visible in some of the six cities in which it operated. One of these was the port of Hoorn, just north of Amsterdam, where a number of house facades have attractive maritime motifs. The VOC memorabilia in the local museum includes the world's oldest share certificate, dating from September 9, 1606, made out to Pieter Harmensz.

Hoorn's most famous son was Willem Schouten, who named Cape Horn after sailing around it in 1616 in search of a Pacific route to the East Indies. Another Hoorn mariner was the much more controversial Jan Coen, the VOC's driving force in its initial forays into Asia. Coen is the 'Clive' of the Netherlands, founder of Batavia, the town he called after the Roman name for one of the Netherlands' Germanic tribes and today corrupted into Jakarta, which has become the capital of Indonesia with a population of ten million. Made Governor-General of the VOC in 1619, Coen was single minded in his attempt to ensure the company controlled all trade between Europe and Asia, attacking any shipping or community that got in the way. His biggest crime against humanity was on the Banda Islands, which possessed the world's only source of nutmeg and mace. When the 15,000 locals refused to offer the VOC sole trading rights, they were either massacred or deported. A statue of this national hero stands in Hoorn's main square. His body remains in Jakarta where he died of disease.

Opposite Hoorn is Lelystad, a town that did not exist in the VOC days: it was founded in the

1970s on land reclaimed from the Zuiderzee. Here is another replica East Indiaman, the *Batavia*. Wrecked off the coast of Western Australia in 1629, she had a lurid history of murder and mutiny. The wreck was explored in the

1970s under the direction of the Western Australian Museum, and the ship was later reconstructed under a work employment programme in Lelystad. In 2000 she was towed to Australia to be the flagship for the Dutch Olympic team at the Sydney Games.

Oost-Indisch Huis, the VOC headquarters in Amsterdam, is still standing. Built in 1606, like East India House it underwent a number of enlargements, but it is essentially a Renaissance building and its canalside position is imposing. Since 1958 it has been occupied by Amsterdam University but the meeting room of the Heeren XVII (the Lords Seventeen), the governing body that was elected from Amsterdam and the other five initiating towns, has been restored. To see such a living reminder of the past only heightens a sense of loss of London's own maritime heritage.

SHIPPING

The City's greatest cluster of 21st-century skyscrapers rises above the few hundred square metres that were once the East India Company's domain. Around Leadenhall Street is the postal district of EC3, the south-east corner of the Square Mile between London Bridge and the Tower. It is the closest the City gets to the sea. This is where the Company's vast warehouses and stores, high walls and wandering alleys shaped the whole layout of the East End of London as it connected along Commercial Road, the highway it built through the Tower hamlets to Poplar and Blackwall, and its India- and China-bound ships.

However, even if a visitor to this quarter of the City had a pint of India Pale Ale at Shepherd Neame's one-room East India Arms in Fenchurch Street, or tried Greene King's Old Tea Clipper Ale over a game of pool in the East India Room of The Old Tea Warehouse in Creechurch Street, he or she would not be much wiser about the crucial place that the Company had occupied.

An idea of the scale of the Company's operations can however be gleaned from a visit to New Street and Devonshire Square on the north side of Leadenhall Street. Here, in an enclosed five-acre complex of six-storey buildings, were the Company's Cutler Street warehouses. In their 21st-century incarnation as a luxury residential and commercial development there is barely a mention of their EIC past, but enough of the original buildings remain to give a sense of their enormous importance.

These warehouses were the destination of cargoes that arrived in London four miles to the east in East India Docks. Once the largest in the world, they were the first of the London docks to close, in 1967. Only a couple of brackish ponds remain but the name resurfaced in 1994 when the Docklands Light Railway was built. The station here was originally to have been called Brunswick Dock, but East India prevailed, ensuring the Company, if only partially, once again found a place on London's maps. The DLR uses track laid  by the London and Blackwall Railway in 1840 by Robert Stephenson to serve the docks. To avoid the potentially incendiary sparks from steam trains, wagons were pulled by cable from a stationary engine at the Minories, its City terminus, now Tower Gateway.

At its height, the Company employed 4,000 in its storage and cargo handling, and it was the business of conveying goods between the docks and the City that shaped London's East End. In the beginning, the Company had embarked on its fortunes from Wool Quay, some 500 metres directly south of Leadenhall Street by the Tower where a system of Legal Quays had been established in Elizabeth's reign. The Wool Quay dated from the 14th century when the King's *troneur* weighed wool for export, overseen by the poet Geoffrey Chaucer who was appointed customs comptroller in 1375. Wool and woollen goods, which the Company optimistically imagined it could sell in Asia, were London's principal export in the early days, and cargoes were initially stored and loaded on this quay. Until the Company's own bonded warehouses began to appear, storage was otherwise found in the Royal Exchange and by Leadenhall Market, and space elsewhere was rented as and when needed.

The Old Custom House was rebuilt by Wren after it was lost in the Great Fire, and it moved a few yards west to its present site in 1814 following another conflagration. This last Custom House, with a dignified Corinthian colonnade by Robert Smirke,

 is the only surviving civic building in the Pool of London that connects directly with the past, still serving its original purpose. Its 190-foot Long Room, with banks of computers, can be seen on Open House

day when sniffer dogs show their tricks. Items such as ivory and exotic animal skins that had been everyday Company merchandise are on display among illegal items on endangered lists that have been caught by Customs officers at Heathrow and other points of entry into London.

The East India Company would have benefited from the use of sniffer dogs. In spite of all efforts, pilfering was rife at every stage of its cargo handling, stages that could not be avoided. Because of their size, East Indiamen had to sit at anchor and rely on hoys and lighters to discharge their cargoes. Avoiding the congestion of the Pool of London, they began to lighten their loads around Gravesend before progressing to Blackwall where barges would take the remaining cargo seven miles upriver to the Legal Quays. Once through customs, goods had to be transported to the City warehouses prior to being auctioned in East India House. One step of this journey was reduced when bonded warehouses were established, bypassing Custom House, but lighters were still needed to unload the ships.

At the time that the Company sold its early interest in Blackwall Yard, it established a presence nearby in Poplar. Here, in quiet and unexciting streets, is the oldest building in Docklands and perhaps the most important memorial to the Company: the East India Company Chapel.

The Company's first building in Poplar was an almshouse, which opened in 1628. The only remaining part of it is Meridian House in Poplar High Street, which was redesigned in 1803 by the Company's Surveyor, Henry Holland, for its Chaplain. The EIC coat of arms with two lions can just be made out on its pediment. The  original institution was the unexpected gift of a miscreant, Hugh Greete. A London jeweller and factor in Borneo, Greete had been sent home a prisoner in 1618 for defrauding the Company in illicit diamond dealing. The following year he died and the Company seized his assets, but his last will and testament expressed his wish for a home to be built for disabled seamen. Having paid off the debt, the Company used the remaining money, adding further funds to establish the almshouse. Thereafter four pence a month was deducted from Company mariners to pay for those disabled in service, a practice that the Royal Navy had already introduced.

At the same time that he built Meridian House,

Holland carried out renovations on the East India Chapel, which stands directly behind it, installing the clock in the distinctive timber turret. Built in 1667 to serve Poplar's growing population, it has since changed its name to St Matthias and become a community centre, which was spruced up in 2015 by 750 hours of free labour donated by contractors of the nearby Crossrail station at Canary Wharf. Its inner space remains a plain Protestant  Latin cross, its aisle roofs supported by eight sturdy pillars, seven of them of oak, the 'seven pillars of Poplar', sometimes said to be former Indiamen's masts. Effusive wall tablets commemorate captains who were loyal servants of the Company. Blackwall shipbuilders are remembered, too: sailing ships decorate George Green's tablet, and John Perry donated the organ. Most colourfully, like a planet twinkling from the distant past, is the ceiling boss with the Company's original coat of arms, a simple device with three ships, celebrating James Lancaster's first voyage. This is undoubtedly the most valuable visible relic of the East India Company in London.

Before the East India Chapel was built, worshippers had to traipse through farmland to All Saints, the ancient parish church of Stepney, later dedicated to St Dunstan, Bishop of London, Archbishop of Canterbury and patron saint of smiths, who held the manor here. Blackwall, Poplar, the marshy Isle of Dogs, Limehouse, Ratcliffe, Shadwell and Wapping: all the Tower hamlets fell within its parish. Ships' captains and merchants were the first to build fine houses among its abundant orchards and cornfields, their harvest festivals celebrated in Dunstan's church where they were married and buried. Predating the Tower of London, it miraculously survived the Blitz, and it has been called 'the mother church of the East End'. Above the west doorway is a ship emblem, while a Red Ensign, flag of the merchant navy, flies from its tower, confirming its other title as 'The Church of the High Seas'. According to its published guide, the minute books of the vestry "*abound with the names of East India Company magnates, ship owners and speculators*".

The 'Sea Captains' Church', on the other hand, was the name given to St Paul's on The Highway at Shadwell, where some seventy-five master mariners are buried. The current church dates from 1820 and incorporates the parish of Ratcliffe, once the centre of shipbuilding on this stretch of river. Deriving its name from its clay 'red cliff', Ratcliffe was the largest of the riverside hamlets at the time that the Company was formed, and ship repairs had already been carried out here for a couple of centuries. As trade increased and marine activities multiplied, these waterfront hamlets began to link up to become one 'Sailortown', rapidly sinking into poverty and squalor as they entered the Victorian age. Shadwell's 'Tiger Bay' became notorious, and the Ratcliffe Highway murders, attributed to a one-time East Indiaman sailor, added to the gruesome images conjured by Charles Dickens and the artist Gustave Doré, and later described in Jack London's 1903 book, *The People of the Abyss*.

Ratcliffe Highway, which ran east from the Tower to Limehouse, was particularly notorious. Today it is just called The Highway, but Ratcliffe's removal from the map has nothing to do with the East India Company blowing it up. Like its neighbouring hamlets, in the 17th and 18th centuries Ratcliffe had a number of handsome riverside properties belonging to merchants and shipping magnates, as well as workers' housing. There were warehouses here, too. Midway between the City and the docks, it was deemed a suitable place to store consignments of saltpetre, used for preserving meat as well as for making gunpowder, and it was one of the Company's more profitable, if volatile, Indian monopolies.

On July 23, 1794 a pitch kettle in Cloves' barge-builder's yard in Stone Stairs spilled, causing a fire that spread to a barge that was unloading a cargo of saltpetre. It was fortunate that half the load, some twenty tons, had been moved to the Tower the day before. Even so, the ensuing conflagration caused massive damage. A description of the event, written a fortnight later, likened it to an earthquake or a volcanic eruption: *"Large flakes of fire fell over the warehouses"*, and *"a vast arch of smoke, white as snow, extended nearly five miles"*. Fuelled by a wind from the south, the fire consumed around fifty-five acres from the waterside to Stepney Causeway, burning without prejudice both slum timber dwellings and elegant merchants' houses.

The following day wardens and officers of the hamlets searched the ruins. Out of 1,200 homes, they estimated that no more than 570 survived, leaving around 2,700 people homeless. Miraculously, there seem to have been no fatalities, though Mr Cloves suffered a broken arm and one of his employees was hospitalised with severe burns. This was said to be the largest conflagration in London since 1666 and not until the 1940 Blitz would its like be seen again. In the Great Fire the Company had enlisted the King's army to help take treasures, books, papers and various goods from East India House to Stepney, and though its Pepper Cellars burned along with the Royal Exchange, the flames did not reach Leadenhall Street. The Ratcliffe explosion allowed no time to rescue anything. The Company did not have insurance, and there were consignments paid for at auction and awaiting collection as well as its own goods that were destroyed. Two saltpetre warehouses were rebuilt, and in the 1980s these were converted into flats. Though Ratcliffe no longer exists, its riverside site is easily recognised

by distinctive twin apartment blocks, bright orange in colour and often described as looking rather like Lego ziggurats.

Ratcliffe Highway, which ran through the heart of Sailortown connecting the riverside hamlets, was not ideal for any kind of heavy-duty transportation, so when the East India Docks were built, the Company, in a joint venture with the West India Dock Company, laid out Commercial Road, just inland, the broad highway leading from Aldgate to Blackwall. This became London's route to docklands and the sea and as the A13 it now follows the Thames all the way to Shrewburyness. Beside it are still a few signs of former seamen's missions and other buildings from the great dock days. After a couple of miles West India Dock Road turns off to the south towards Canary Wharf while Commercial Road continues as the East India Dock Road. Here, outside the newly rebuilt Poplar

Baths, is a bronze statue by Edward Wyon of the shipbuilder Richard Green with his Newfoundland  hound Hector. The East Indiamen he built are depicted around the base. The son of Sarah Perry and George Green, who took over the management of the Blackwall yard in 1820, Richard followed his father into the business, developing the Blackwall Frigates. He also continued the philanthropic work of his father, funding a mission, school and hospital, and building Trinity Chapel where, in 1849 and 1863, they were buried. Supported by the Worshipful Company of Shipwrights, the George Green School is thriving, as is the Queen Victoria Seamen's Rest, successor to Green's Sailors' Home, but the Chapel was bombed in 1944.

Just beyond the Baths, the road crosses the A12 as it disappears beneath Blackwall Tunnel. Around here was the entrance to the East India Docks, which had opened to a great fanfare in 1806. The inscribed foundation stones are preserved in a large brick wall on the south-east side of this junction:

"...They were opened by the introduction of five ships from 1,200 to 800 tons with valuable cargoes from IV August MDCCCVI. The grand undertaking originated in the laudable endeavours of the owners of ships in the company's service and the important national objects of increased security to property and revenue, combined with improved accommodation and despatch were thus early realised..."

An extension to the Brunswick Dock, the East India Docks were created by a consortium of merchants and yard owners, Company men who could see the evident success of the West India Dock Company, which had just been completed.

Covering some thirty acres, the East India Docks held a monopoly on the Asia trade for twenty-one years. A tranche of the outer dock wall stands near the river in Naval Row. Impenetrable except through a couple of small metal gates, this fortress curtain  is still impressive and retains an air of security, if not exclusivity. Behind it is the East India Dock Estate, a nine-acre development of large office blocks. Thin, architect-designed water courses  follow Nutmeg Lane, Saffron Avenue and Oregano Drive to what is left of the Import Dock. All signs of industry have been washed away. The Export Dock has long since been filled in, and a footbridge via East India DLR station is the only way to cross the A1261 dual carriageway to reach the Dock Basin. Looking across Blackwall Reach to the O2 Arena, this one-time gateway to the East is protected by a lock, and its brackish water offers a habitat of saltmarsh, shingle, reedbeds and mudflats. Rafts attract nesting terns from May to July.

 Beyond the Basin is Bow Creek on the River Lea, the border in the Company's day between Middlesex and Essex. Trinity Buoy Wharf, a 19th-century industrial precinct that Trinity House made its base for repairing and storing buoys at the same time that the East India Docks were built. An experimental lighthouse is still standing,

a beacon for creative arts projects, but this land's end can still evoke the dock days of Poplar.

A short distance up the River Lea at Bow Bridge, George Hodgson set up a brewery to supply the ships, inadvertently discovering that October brews matured quickly on the warm passage to India. His virtual monopoly lasted some forty years until a ban by Russia on trade meant a loss of orders for the brewers of Burton-on-Trent. Offering more favourable credit incentives, the Staffordshire brewers developed the heavily hopped India Pale Ales especially for the Company. IPA has undergone a revival in recent years with London's many micro brewers and brewpubs.

Although it had some storage space for low-value bulk goods, the Company had no need of vast dockside warehousing, as it had its own bonded warehouses in the City, and cargoes could be taken straight from the docks along Commercial Road to Aldgate and Cutler Street. Even so, vigilance had to be maintained. Armed guards accompanied convoys of hired horse-drawn wagons, their cargoes often padlocked in early containers.

The Cutler Street warehouses were the most extensive of any business in London. The first of these, designed in 1770 by the Company's architect, Richard Jupp, were the Old Bengal and Tapestry Warehouses in New Street, opposite Liverpool Street Station, now places to wine and dine. Beside them is the main complex of six-storey blocks, enclosed with gates and high boundary walls, completed in 1808 by Jupp's successors Henry Holland, a pioneer of the use of fireproof construction, and Samuel Pepys Cockerell. Without steam or electricity, goods had to be hauled up to every floor by hand. The greatest chunk of Georgian industrial architecture in the City was saved through continued use. When the Company lost its monopoly on the China trade in 1833, it

was forced to sell its property. The Cutler Street warehouses were taken over first by St Katharine Docks, then by the Port of London Authority to cater for the most valuable cargoes of the burgeoning British Empire. Its warehousemen were so knowledgeable about textiles, minerals, drugs and other imports, that they would be consulted by museum curators and academics. In 1914, the cornucopia of Cutler Street opened the eyes of the Poet Laureate John Masefield:

"You showed me nutmegs and nutmeg husks,
Ostrich feathers and elephant tusks
Hundreds of tons of costly tea
Packed in wood by the Cingalee
And a myriad drugs which disagree
Cinnamon, myrrh and mace you showed
Golden paradise birds that glowed
And a billion cloves in an odorous mount
And choice port wine from a bright glass fount
You showed, for a most delightful hour
The wealth of the world, and London's power."

Containerisation put warehouses out of business, and it also put paid to pilfering. Beside Cutler Street's eastern boundary is Middlesex Street, known as Petticoat Lane, where a market was once notorious for selling stolen goods. A visitor's watch might be pickpocketed at one end, it was said, and sold back to him at the other. Prosecutions for theft from the East India Company were not infrequent, and the Old Bailey's records show several cases each year brought by the Company, which would result in whippings, incarceration and, on rare occasions, transportation. In 1978 the Cutler Street warehouses were sold to Standard Life and Greycoat Development. The sale caused preservation societies to rally to try to save 'the finest group of early industrial buildings in London'. In a campaigning brochure the architectural historian Marc Girouard wrote:

"The East India Company warehouses in Cutler Street are both evocative and romantic. They form an enormous complex of buildings; courtyard leads into courtyard, great walls of brown brick rise above cobbled yards, dark and mysterious tunnels are cut through the lush facades to lead to yet more courts. At regular intervals ruggedly simple stone stairs rise up, in apparently limitless vistas, to great warehouse lofts. In these long perspectives, massively rough-hewn timber posts support equally massive brackets and beams with lines of exposed joists between them. It is a hierarchy of timber construction that is entirely satisfying because it is so solid and workmanlike. There is the same feeling about the details throughout the building from the cast-iron panels on which are incised the names of the various courts to the cyclopean rustication of the occasional stretches of ashlar stonework.

"It is all intensely evocative of the days when wagons rumbled through the archways fresh from the East Indiamen in the docks, and the warehouses were piled high with all the stuffs and spices of the East."

In 2003 Margaret Makepeace, Lead Curator, East India Company Records, at the British Library and author of *The East India Company's London Workers: Management of the Warehouse Labourers, 1800-1858*, had a glimpse of the past when she visited the Old Bengal Warehouse in New Street, the oldest part of the complex, then called Shield House. "The last East India Company warehouse in London was in something very close to its original state," she says. "It was built in the mid-18th century to store muslins, calicoes, raw and wrought silks, and shawls shipped to London from Bengal. Work was about to begin to convert it for residential and retail use. I was able to stand in the empty warehouse rooms and imagine what it was like when they were filled with bales of cloth and labourers busy about their work. Fireproof metal doors with large bolts separated the floors into large compartments with low ceilings broken up only by columns to help load bearing. I was one of the last outsiders to gain access before modernisation."

Architects of the new estate were R. Seifert and Partners, and a mix of refurbishment meant twelve Grade II listed buildings were retained and new six-storey blocks replaced those pulled down on the east side, beside Middlesex Street, where the dramatic, blind brick warehouse wall was demolished. A clock and fire bell were salvaged from the old clock tower and a glass canopy was added to keep the weather out of a quadrangle of original buildings in the West Courtyard. Adopting the name of the adjacent Devonshire Square, abbreviated to DSQ, it created a secure 'campus environment' of 'executive flats', served with gyms and squash courts and encouraging community activity. Animated by

food stalls on weekday lunchtimes, and musicians in summer, this private enclave is one of the City's increasing number of island enclosures. It is easier to imagine the Company's cargoes incarcerated within these secure walls at night when the gates are locked and guarded, and the CCTVs keep their vigils. Londoners who may come for an Indian meal here at the Cinnamon Kitchen, or to enjoy a cocktail in the Old Bengal Bar, find little information about the buildings' past. In searching for a symbol to trumpet the regeneration, the developers ignored the exotic products, the ships and the East India Company, choosing instead a figure with a different connection to London's docks. The equestrian sculpture of a knight in armour, commissioned from the St Ives artist Denys Mitchell is designed to celebrate the grant of 'this derelict land' given to thirteen knights by King Edgar in the tenth century. The land extended southwards into the Thames "*as far as a horseman riding into the river at low tide can throw a lance*". There is no mention that several acres of this riverside estate were then donated to Queen Matilda, wife of King Stephen, to build the Royal Hospital and Collegiate Church of St Katharine by the Tower. The land would be acquired

in 1825 under an Act of Parliament by the St Katharine Docks Company. The hospital and its church were then demolished, along with 1,250 houses, to make way for Thomas Telford's St Katharine Docks. The Royal Foundation of St Katharine eventually came to rest in Butcher Row in Limehouse where it still offers accommodation and retreat.

LASCARS AND AYAHS

Through a global network of chaplains, staff and volunteers, the Mission to Seafarers attempts to look after some of the 1.5 million employed on merchant ships around the world. Its head office is in St Michael Paternoster Royal, College Hill in the City, the church where the philanthropic Dick Whittington, three times Lord Mayor of London, is buried.

The Mission has its work cut out. In spite of efforts from national and international labour unions, seamen have little protection or rights. They may work around the clock, be poorly fed, go unpaid, be abused, enslaved and become victims of pirate attacks. Every year around 10,000 containers go missing and 2,000 sailors die at sea. In *Deep Sea and Foreign Going*, an account of a container ship voyage to Singapore, the journalist Rose George brings these depressing facts to light. The book was originally titled *Ninety Percent of Everything*, based on George's realisation that whether she was indoors, in the street or travelling, ninety percent of everything she saw – buildings, transportation, clothes, furniture, food – had been on a ship. This is a complete inversion of the world in which the East India Company embarked, when just about everything that surrounded people in Britain was home made. It was a world the Company turned upside down.

Today, as then, many sailors come from Asia,

though Russians and East Europeans have been added to the polyglot crews. In the world of the East India Company, whatever Asian country a seaman came from, and whatever god he worshipped, he was called simply a *lascar*, a word that seems to have been taken from the Persian for soldier, first used in Europe by the Portuguese.

English merchant seamen were recruited from among the rogues and poor of London. For all its terror and hardships, life at sea meant an escape from hunger, a prospect often faced at home, and sometimes it meant an escape from the law. Of course there was also the possibility of making some money. Discipline was less severe than in the Royal Navy; it was entirely in a ship's interest to have a full and healthy working crew. But the attrition wrought by the journeys meant that often there was a shortage of hands to bring the ships home, so locals were sought and pressed into service. Starvation would have been a driving force in Asia, too.

The manning of ships by lascars was the subject of constant adjustment. A Navigation Act passed in 1660 restricted the employment of non-English seamen on returning East India Company ships to a quarter of the crew. Lascars suffered mixed fortunes. Many were preyed on in London and lost what little money they had. Often arriving in the autumn, and having to wait until the next season's sailing, without proper lodgings and little food, some succumbed to the cold. A few were spared the hardships of England when they were transferred from homeward bound to outward bound ships before reaching Gravesend. Cooks were often highly regarded, especially Goans, and they might make several journeys under a particular captain who appreciated their cuisine.

Some even took to the seaman's life for a while, making several trips and taking home cheap souvenirs for their families and friends. But most had a pretty miserable time, waiting for the next available ship out and hoping for a berth, when they would travel as passengers. Under a later Navigation Act, they were not allowed to work their passage home, but they still had to face the hazards of the journey. In December 1810 scores of lascars and several *ayahs* perished in a wreck off Dunkirk, along with most of the rest of the passengers and crew on the *Elizabeth*, which had spent two months trying to get out of the English Channel.

Lascars were on the whole deemed unsuited for seamanship, and the Company estimated that one European sailor was worth two of them, a figure it later adjusted to three. Now and then they mutinied, but lack of navigational skills could be a bar to taking over a ship. The Company made little effort to look after them once in London, contending that they were the liability of the ships 'husbands' or charterers. Responsibility was usually passed to the *serangs* and their junior *tindals*, the Indian officers in charge of the lascar crews, who were given funds to ensure their welfare, but they themselves were not beyond fleecing their charges.

By the end of the 18th century lascars had become a common sight in east London, and if there was any trouble among them, or with locals, people would blame the Company for bringing them here. So the Company began to look for suitable accommodation, sending them first to Charles Eyloe's Orchard House in Blackwall, where Trinity Wharf now lies, while from 1797 Mrs Susannah Smetza in Kingsland Road and Mrs Coates in

Hackney Road were contracted to take them in. In 1801 fights among Chinese and other lascars broke out around Kingsland Road, causing public disquiet, and the Company felt compelled to respond. They turned to a Chinese Christian, who had worked for them as an interpreter, to set up a Depot in Angel Gardens in Shadwell to feed, clothe and look after the lascars, who would be met off ships by his carts. Known to history and to the parliamentary records only as John Anthony, he did well financially from the arrangement and married Sarah Gole, becoming Britain's first naturalised Chinese, an occasion that necessitated an Act of Parliament. On his death in 1805 at the age of thirty-nine, the Depot was taken over by his father-in-law, Abraham Gole, and his brother-in-law, also called Abraham, who built further barracks on Cannon Street Road.

Lascars still found lodgings where they could elsewhere, and if possible some even remained on board ship where they would be guaranteed something to eat. The number of lascars maintained by the Company hit a peak of 1,403 in 1810 during the Napoleonic Wars, when British merchant sailors were being pressed into the Royal Navy. Between May 1813 and May 1814 122 lascars are reported to have died in the Shadwell Depot. Illiterate and not eligible for a churchyard burial, they have left no trace.

Observations on the State of Society among the Asiatic Subjects of Great Britain, published in 1792 and widely read, brought the place of lascars in London into focus. It was written by Charles Grant, who had served in Calcutta and become Chairman of the Board of Governors in Leadenhall Street in 1905. He believed India had been delivered to

Britain by God in order to bring the light of the Almighty's truth into this world of darkness. It was an idea that caught fire and brought about a sea-change in the Company when Grant joined William Wilberforce in getting Parliament to pass the 'Pious Clause' of 1813 that finally allowed Company ships to take missionaries to India. Grant was also a social reformer, opposed to Wellesley's military advances in India and the practice of *sati*, the ritual immolation of women on the death of their husbands. A monument to him in St George's Bloomsbury was paid for by the Company.

Full responsibility for lascars' welfare was not accepted by the Company until obliged to by law in 1823, but when its trading monopoly was wound up ten years later, its responsibility came to an end and Shadwell Depot went out of business. The baton was passed to East India Dock manager George Green who opened the 200-bed Sailors' Home in East India Dock Road in 1841. Popularly known as Green's, it took in all nationalities. By this time evangelising missionaries were not only going to Asia, they were spreading through the destitute streets of London, too. Most effective of the East End missions was the London City Mission, which today has its headquarters in Tooley Street by London Bridge, and the slogan 'London needs Jesus'. Begun in Hoxton in 1835, its volunteers established Ragged Schools in the East End and were involved with R. M. Hughes, a former East India Company army officer, in establishing the Strangers' Home for Asiatics, Africans and South Sea Islanders, a large hostel in Limehouse to which the Company

contributed financially, as did Maharajah Duleep Singh. Prince Albert laid the first stone in 1856.

Six years later, Captain Superintendent George Smith, RN, wrote in *The Evangelical Christian and Temperance Sailors and Soldiers' Magazine*: "*Walked through Poplar and gave tracts to the Strangers House, the large building in the high road that is now established for coloured Lascars and Chinese sailors. Glory be to God, I well recollect the horrors I witnessed, for years, at the East India Dock, where these poor foreign sailors were left out of each ship as they arrived from India or China, and had to sleep on the ground, in the most wretched shed.*"

It was the Strangers' Mission that brought Limehouse the reputation of being 'Oriental London', London's first Chinese quarter where Sherlock Holmes visited opium dens and where Sax Rohmer's evil Fu Manchu roamed. But the Chinese population here was never large, and certainly no bigger than the Irish, Caribbean or Scandinavian. It was only after the Second World War, which destroyed so much of Docklands, that a Chinatown began to surface, not by the river but in Soho.

The Norwegian mission is still active in St Olave's in Rotherhithe, where Surrey Docks catered for the Baltic trade, and there are Finnish and Swedish mission churches nearby. Otherwise there are few glimpses of

the major role missions have played in London's maritime story. The huge Empire Mission opposite the old Limehouse Town Hall, for example, was built after the First World War and is being converted into flats.

The London City Mission also ran a home for ayahs. Many of these Asian nannies and maids, who accompanied families home from India, also suffered the bewilderment and privations of being dumped, and although their employers had been obliged to pay for their round trip, they often had difficulties in finding a passage home. The first ayahs' house was established in Jewry Street, Aldgate, by concerned English women and run by

a Mrs Rogers. Increase in the number of families travelling East under the Raj led to the London City Mission taking over from the Jewry Street establishment and setting up the Ayahs' Home at 26 King Edward's Road in Hackney, a double-fronted four-storey building, now flats. Their experience is related in a corner of the nearby Hackney Library and Museum, where it tells how an ayah known as Mrs Antony Pareira was employed on more than fifty voyages. Like travelling servants in England, she was presumably given the name of her employer.

Hackney was also where the Company set up Pembroke House where it sent employees who had been driven insane in the East. Here, in 1818, under Dr Rees of 49 Finsbury Square, *"Three-fourths of those admitted"* were *"restored to health and reason"*. Patients were expected to reimburse the Company with the doctor's fees once they were released.

As for ayahs, tickets for their return passages would be given up to the management of the Ayahs' Home. The tickets would then be sold to families heading east who would employ the ayah, and the money would go towards paying for care in the home. Some ayahs would remain with the family in England, and a few, like Mrs Pareira, made a business of travelling back and forth. But as with the lascars it is impossible to generalise and hard to know the full stories. As illiterate as most of the English sailors, with the added complication of names that were either very similar or made up, the stories of those who arrived on East Indiamen have vanished without trace.

What is clear, however, is that abuse of cheap labour both at sea and among the employers of domestic immigrant staff was one monopoly the Company never acquired. It is a universal plight that is with us still.

DOWNRIVER

There is a sweeping view of the Thames from Windmill Hill in Gravesend. At 180 feet above sea level it is little more than half the height of the Shard but it looks out over the flatlands of Kent and Essex, and if the panorama diagram displayed there is to be believed, on a clear day when the oak trees are not in leaf there is a vista stretching from Canary Wharf to Southend. Built on a chalk spur topped with Thanet sand and pebble beds, Gravesend is where the marshy estuary narrows to the 'throat' of the Thames, the halfway point between the city and the sea: some twenty miles either way, one tide distant. Henry VIII had blockhouses built at Gravesend and at Tilbury on the opposite bank, and when the Spanish Armada threatened, London was protected from a sea invasion by a boom of masts and chains laid across the river between the two.

Some like to say that Gravesend derives its name from the fact that this was the limit to where anybody dying on board a ship had to be buried in hallowed ground. From here on down to the estuary, they could be wrapped in sailcloth, weighed down with a cannonball

and heaved over the side, with no memorial but a mention in the ship's log. Suffering a fatal illness, the twenty-two-year-old Native American Princess Pocahontas was on her way back to Virginia when she was saved from a watery grave. Brought ashore at Gravesend, she died and was buried in the chancel of St George's church.

Gravesend was the first port of call for incoming vessels, which might arrive in some numbers after waiting for a fair wind to bring them up the estuary from the Downs. East Indiamen would hove to along these reaches to unburden their bulkiest cargoes. Erith, Purfleet, Greenhithe all played their part in the maritime trade, but it was at Gravesend that ships had to stop to allow Customs Searchers to come on board to assess duties payable. Estuary Pilots would hand over to River Pilots, and Tide Waiters would sail with the ships up to the legal quays to ensure nothing went astray. There was a quarantine check, too, and captains had to swear on a 'plague bible' that there was no disease on board.

Flitting among merchantmen, fishing boats, hoys and barges were the 'tilts', small sailing boats with awnings that took cross-Channel passengers arriving by road from Dover on the last stretch to London, avoiding the highwaymen of Blackheath and providing a less bumpy end to their journey.

Activity in the town intensified as the annual sailing season to Asia approached, and East Indiamen came down from Blackwall to prepare for their six months at sea, mooring in midstream all along Gravesend Reach and Northfleet Hope. Here they would remain for up to a month while they took on board all they required, from personnel and personal items for private trade to ballast, cargo and livestock. Each ship might require a hundred tons of provisions, including large quantities of beer and wine to counter the forty tons or so of foul Thames water that was taken on board for drinking. Animals were embarked, and among the more unlikely sights were hunting hounds, the first pack shipping out to India in 1772.

No commander of an East Indiaman ever wrote his memoirs, but in *Newton Forster* (1832), the pioneering writer of naval fiction Captain Frederick Marryat describes the 'farmyard' on the 1,200-ton East Indiaman *Bombay Castle* as she lay at Gravesend preparing to sail.

"The poop, upon which you ascended by ladders on each side, was crowded with long ranges of coops, tenanted by every variety of domestic fowl, awaiting in happy unconsciousness the day when they should be required to supply the luxurious table provided by the captain. In some, turkeys stretched forth their long necks, and tapped the decks as they picked up some ant who crossed it. In others, the crowing of cocks and calling of the hens were incessant: or the geese, ranged up rank and file, waited for the signal from one of the party to raise up a simultaneous clamour, which as suddenly was remitted. Coop answered coop, in variety of discord, while the poulterer walked round and round to supply the wants of so many hundreds committed to his charge.

"The booms before the main-mast were occupied by the large boats, which had been hoisted in preparatory to the voyage. They also composed a portion of the farm yard. The launch contained about fifty sheep, wedged together so close that it was with difficulty they could

find room to twist their jaws round, as they chewed the cud. The stern-sheets of the barge and yawl were filled with goats and two calves, who were the first destined victims to the butcher's knife; while the remainder of their space was occupied by hay and other provender, pressed down by powerful machinery into the smallest compass. The occasional baa-ing and bleating on the booms were answered by the lowing of three milch-cows between the hatchways of the deck below; where also were to be descried a few more coops, containing fowls and rabbits. The manger forward had been dedicated to the pigs; but, as the cables were not yet unbent or bucklers shipped, they at present were confined by gratings between the main-deck guns, where they grunted at each passer-by, as if to ask for food."

Boats hoisted on davits became 'kitchen gardens' laden with onions, turnips, potatoes, carrots, beets and cabbages, which was all good business for farmers in Kent. But not everything in the Garden of England was lovely. In his 1792 book *Picturesque Views on the River Thames* Samuel Ireland wrote of Gravesend: "*The first port on our river is well situated for commerce, and is famed for fish, filth, and asparagus.*"

Today Gravesend is a clean and tidy place, and local asparagus is sold in a Farmers' Market on the second Friday of each month. Saris, Indian jewellery, haberdashery and cheap trinkets are otherwise the main merchandise in the daily market that occupies the Old Town Hall, a grand neoclassical building that expresses civic ambitions that have long since shrunk.

The business of stowing goods and victuals on East Indiamen was generally handled by the boatswain, and although the commander might put in an occasional appearance, his job did not start until the day before departure when the crew was given two months' pay. EIC army recruits would board then, too, many from a camp on the East India Field behind what is now the Gravesend Yacht Club and Marina. The fields have long since been built on, and nobody in the town recognises the name today. Gone, too, is the Company hospital in Sussex Place where from 1812 the Resident Surgeon inspected the health of all lascars on both outward- and homeward-bound ships.

In the days of sail and the early days of steam, wharfs were busy and so were the inns. Ocean travellers spent their last nights in England here, and taverns stretched along The Shore on the western side of the town at Northfleet. One of the most prominent was The India Arms Tavern, once a base for the Company, opened in 1780 and closed in 1978. Northfleet riverside is now an industrial area, a sea of grey sheds barring access to the river, but there had long been small-scale boat building around Ebbsfleet Creek. The invention of Portland cement at the end of the 18th century created a new demand for chalk, with a result that the whole waterfront was quarried, opening up as the cliff face withdrew. Thomas Pitcher from Deptford initiated the most important of these yards in 1788 to become one of the largest on the river. The first of around three dozen East Indiamen to slip into the water from Pitcher's Yard was the *Royal Charlotte* and a model from that time sits in a glass case in the medieval church of St Botolph, which stands on  an inland promontory above a chalk ravine caused by the quarrying. Chalk provided ships' ballast, and the pits found other uses, as Victorian leisure gardens and a location for the Bluewater shopping centre. In 2007 a tunnel arrived among the chalk pits from beneath the Thames to  bring the high-speed train from St Pancras in less than twenty minutes en route for Paris, stopping at the freshly minted Ebbsfleet station where a new town has been promised.

The Company lasted long enough to see the changes that were rung in Victorian times when day trippers from London began arriving on paddle steamers. The first pleasure seekers disembarked  in 1815 at Gravesend's Town Quay. This is the heart of the old waterfront where the atmospheric Three Daws has been in business since the 15th century. Knocked up by ships' carpenters, its timbers are idiosyncratic, its floorboards creak and of course there are rumours of secret passages used by smugglers and by sailors evading press gangs. The pub no longer offers accommodation, but many a man on Company business would have stayed here.

What the early day trippers, as well as sailors, found on arrival at Gravesend were shrimp and watercress stalls, tea gardens with mazes, archery butts and 'gipsy tents'. Clifton Spa was built along fashionable Moghul lines to echo Brighton's Pavilion, and from Town Quay a road led up to Windmill Gardens on Windmill Hill where there were donkey rides and a view projected on to a *camera obscura*. Town Pier, the world's oldest surviving cast-iron pier, opened in 1834. It now has a smart restaurant and a jetty to the ferry that ploughs back and forth to Tilbury opposite.

Royal Terrace Pier, a short walk east, was given its regal title when nineteen-year-old Princess Alexandra of Denmark landed here to be greeted by her betrothed, Bertie, the Prince of Wales, the future Edward VII. Her wedding gift from her mother-in-law, Queen Victoria, Empress of India, was the Indian Necklace, a suite of collar, armlet and two bracelets, made from uncut emeralds, diamonds and pearls. Since the late 19th century Royal Terrace Pier has been owned by the Port of London Authority, which provides River Pilots and monitors the 38,000 shipping movements on the Thames each year. Custom House, a hundred yards away, is still in use. Customs men have been here since the 14th century, and this building dates from 1815. It has a lookout on the roof where a telescope could spot traffic as far away as the entrance to the Thames at the Nore.

Today there is a new landmark, the Guru Nanak Darbar Gurdwara Sikh Temple. This glorious white-domed building, clad in pristine Kota granite and marble from India, opened in 2010 and all visitors are welcome. Gravesend's large  Sikh population raised the money for the temple's construction, and dedicated it to the victims of the massacre at Amritsar – not the one in 1919 when hundreds of unarmed civilians were mowed down by the British under Brigadier-General Reginald Dyer, but the one in 1984 when Indian troops, advised by the British SAS, stormed the Golden Temple. Sikhs were a significant part of the British Indian Army in both world wars but their arrival in Gravesend dates from the 1950s. Although they cannot be traced directly back to the East India Company, that is where the seeds of their immigration began and where the shadows of their past remain.

Between 1845 and 1849 the Company waged two wars against the Sikhs in the Punjab, which brought young Duleep Singh, the last Maharajah of India, and the Koh-i-Noor diamond to Britain. Courted by Queen Victoria, he converted to Christianity and lived at Elveden Hall in Suffolk, refurbishing its interior to seem more like a Mughal palace. In later life, resentment about his lost inheritance set in and he reverted to Sikhism. Attempting to return to Lahore on March 30, 1886, he and his family boarded SS *Verona* at Gravesend but he was arrested by the British in Aden, and exiled to Paris where six years later he died in penury. The government felt the need to immortalise him as a Christian, so they brought his body back to Elveden where he was buried in the church of St Andrew and St Patrick. Elveden Hall passed into the hands of the Guinness family and in 1999 Queen Victoria's great-great-great grandson, Prince Charles, unveiled a fine equestrian statue of Duleep Singh in nearby Thetford, a train journey of around two hours from London. "*To this day*" the inscription ends, "*the Sikh nation aspires to regain its sovereignty.*"

The hopes of many have sprung from Gravesend. Today the town itself aspires to be a modern, amenable place to live and work. No longer rich but getting by, it pitches commercial interests against a sense of the past. In 2015 a £125-million development plan for the 'Heritage Quarter' was given the go-ahead. This is its maritime heart, around Town Pier, less than ten minutes' walk from the railway station and the first port of call on any visit, and it certainly makes a pleasant day out from London.

To the east, beyond Royal Terrace Pier, the grassy promenade provides the ideal spot to sit and watch the river traffic, the cruise liners and container ships, ro-ro ferries and freighters, pilot boats, leisure yachts, tugs and Thames barges. There may be no sign left of the Honourable East India Company's last anchorage in England, but ships still evoke thoughts of travel, of new sights and experiences, of chance and life changes, and it is hard sitting here on a bright, breezy day not to imagine the clank of anchor chains, the slap of hemp ropes against the masts and the crump of unfolding canvas as sailors on the yardarms of the East Indiamen set the sails and begin to make headway towards their journeys of adventure and exploitation. For the many who never returned, this would be where they took their last steps on English soil.

INDEX

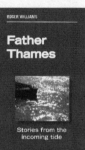